# Holy Spirit 101

## Other Books in the *101 Series*

**Mary 101**
*Tradition and Influence*
Mary Ann Zimmer

**Jesus 101**
*God and Man*
John L. Gresham

**Scripture 101**
*An Intro to Reading the Bible*
William J. Parker, C.Ss.R.

**Church History 101**
*A Concise Overview*
Christopher M. Bellitto PhD

**Liturgy 101**
*Sacraments and Sacramentals*
Daniel G. Van Slyke, STL, PhD

To order visit your local bookstore
or call 800-325-9521 or visit us at www.liguori.org

# Holy Spirit 101
## Present Among Us

JOHN L. GRESHAM, PhD

Liguori
ONE LIGUORI DRIVE
LIGUORI MO 63057-9999

Imprimi Potest:
Harry Grile, CSsR, Provincial
Denver Province, The Redemptorists

Imprimatur: "In accordance with c. 827, permission to publish has been granted on July 5, 2011, by the Most Reverend Robert J. Hermann, Auxiliary Bishop Emeritus, Archdiocese of St. Louis. Permission to publish is an indication that nothing contrary to Church teaching is contained in this work. It does not imply any endorsement of the opinions expressed in the publication; nor is any liability assumed by this permission."

Published by Liguori Publications, Liguori, Missouri 63057
To order, call 800-325-9521, or visit liguori.org

### Library of Congress Cataloging-in-Publication Data

Gresham, John Leroy.
  Holy Spirit 101 : present among us / John L. Gresham.
    p. cm.
  Includes bibliographical references.
  ISBN 978-0-7648-1985-8
  1. Holy Spirit. 2. Catholic Church—Doctrines. I. Title. II. Title: Holy Spirit one hundred one.
  BT121.3.G753 2011
  231'.3—dc23

                    2011023399

Compliant with *The Roman Missal*, third edition.

"Fresh Fire" from *My Journey to the Land of More* by Leona Choy. 2010, CHResources, Zanesville, OH.

Printed in the United States of America
15 14 13 12 11  /  5 4 3 2 1
First Edition

*To my children, each one a special gift from God:*
*Hannah, Sarah, Rebekah, Katie, and John Daniel*

∼

*I am also deeply grateful to Tim Dallas, Jane Guenther, and Mark Reasoner for reading this text and for their helpful suggestions. Thanks also to Leona Choy for permission to use her poem prayer "Fresh Fire." Because prayer is so important to knowing the Holy Spirit, this book begins with prayer. Please make this your prayer each time you open this book.*

# Contents

# About This Book

The primary sources for this book on the Holy Spirit are sacred Scripture, the *Catechism of the Catholic Church*, and the writings of Blessed John Paul II .

Scripture references are given in parentheses, and readers are encouraged to read this book alongside an open Bible.

The citations to the *Catechism of the Catholic Church* are also given. As an organic synthesis of our faith, the catechism is like a fountain of truth from which you can drink again and again.

References to papal encyclicals are cited by title and paragraph number. John Paul II's general audiences are cited by the date (month/day/year), except for his audiences on *Theology of the Body,* which are cited by paragraph number.

# Introduction

When Saint Paul arrived in Ephesus, he encountered some disciples, but apparently noticed that there was something missing in their religious experience. He asked them, "Did you receive the Holy Spirit...?" They replied, "No, we have not even heard that there is a Holy Spirit" (Acts 19:1–2). Almost nineteen hundred years later, in his encyclical on the Holy Spirit, Pope Leo XIII wondered if there were Catholics in his day who might reply to Saint Paul's query in the same way. Of course, these Catholics could recite the Creed and say, "I believe in the Holy Spirit," but the question is how well do they know the Holy Spirit? How intimate is their relationship to this divine person? It is still a valid question. Most Catholics know something of the Spirit but would like to know him better. This book is designed to help Catholics grow toward a fuller knowledge of the Spirit, a deeper intimacy in their relationship with him, and a greater receptivity to his gifts.

Knowledge of the Spirit must be experiential. You cannot study the wind by capturing it in a jar and bringing it into the lab for examination. Still less can we capture the Spirit. The wind of the Spirit does not sit still for a merely academic investigation. Those who understand wind the best are sailors, wind surfers, and hang gliders, those who learn to move with the wind, those who allow the wind to carry them over water and through the sky. Likewise, those who best understand the Spirit are those who surrender to the power of the Spirit and allow the Spirit to carry them forward in the spiritual journey of greater love for God and service to others. This book is written as an invitation for readers to open themselves to the movement of the Spirit. I encourage readers to accompany their reading of this book with frequent prayers to the Holy Spirit, welcoming this "Holy Guest" into their hearts, their minds, and their lives.

# Fresh Fire

### BY LEONA CHOY

*Veni Sancte Spiritus*
Come, Holy Spirit
descend on me with FRESH FIRE
flames of Pentecost, tongues of FIRE
fall upon and fill me
renew my stony heart to flesh
purify my soul
burn away the dross of self.

O Holy Spirit of God
Light Your Church AFIRE
transform us to burning bushes
yet not consumed, living sacrifices
touch our lips with glowing coals until
we are fully possessed by You
to speak holy words, think holy thoughts

We see reflected in Your holy FIRE
the brilliance of Your Manifest Presence
let the flames of Your searing love
blaze fiercely on the altars of our hearts
never quenched, never diminished
a perpetual sacrifice of praise
as fragrant incense rising to God's throne.

O Spirit, impart to me a burning heart
as I walk with Christ on my Emmaus road
fan the embers of my passion
back to "first love" intensity.

O Spirit, endue Your Church with holy power
to spread Your FIRE abroad
and ignite the Final Harvest Fields ablaze
to rescue rebellious mankind
from the kingdom of darkness
to Your brilliant kingdom of light
by Your uncommon FIRE!

# CHAPTER 1

# The Mystery of the Spirit in Names, Titles, and Symbols

## *The Mystery of the Holy Spirit*

In the Nicene Creed, we confess our faith in the three persons of the Holy Trinity. We believe in one God: the Father, the Son, and the Holy Spirit. Of these three divine persons, the Holy Spirit is the most mysterious to most of us. We have human fathers: biological fathers, adoptive fathers, or spiritual fathers, the best of whom point us to the mystery of our heavenly Father. We can get some concrete idea of what God the Father is like. While we know the reality of God transcends any such images, we can picture the first person of the Trinity as the white-bearded father in heaven, as he is often depicted in Christian art. Likewise, the second person of the Trinity, the Son, is accessible to us through many human images.

The eternal Son of the Father was incarnate as man, and we can know him as revealed in his human nature. We can read about his life in the Gospels, contemplate his face depicted in icons, venerate his image on the crucifix, and adore his sacred heart. Both Father and Son are accessible to our understanding and imagination in these concrete human images. The third person of the Holy Trinity, the Holy Spirit, is another matter altogether. He appears as a dove, as fire, as wind. He is poured out like water or descends like rain. His presence is invisible, hidden, sometimes powerful, but often very quiet and imperceptible. When it comes to the Holy Spirit, we lack the concrete human images that help us to understand the Father and the Son.

However mysterious he may be to us, it is absolutely essential to our spiritual life that we come to know the Holy Spirit. It is only through the Holy Spirit that we come to have faith in Jesus Christ the Son, and it is by the Holy Spirit that we learn to call upon the Father in faith and love (CCC 152, 683). As "the master of prayer" who teaches and guides us into intimacy with God, the Holy Spirit is our indispensable teacher in the spiritual life (CCC 741, 2672). It is the Holy Spirit who heals the wounds of sin, renews us interiorly, enlightens us, and strengthens us for a life of goodness and charity (CCC 1695). We cannot live the Christian life without the aid of the Holy Spirit. Despite the difficulty in understanding this mysterious divine person, if we are to progress in Christian prayer and living, it is essential that we come to know him.

### Last to be Revealed

The catechism provides a couple of reasons why the Holy Spirit is so mysterious. In explaining these reasons, the catechism also points the way toward a better understanding of this mysterious divine person. The first reason is chronological. The Holy Spirit is the last of the three persons of the Trinity to be fully revealed and known as a person. As Saint Gregory of Nazianzus explains, "The Old Testament proclaimed the Father clearly, but the Son more obscurely. The New Testament revealed the Son and gave us a glimpse of the divinity of the Spirit. Now the Spirit dwells among us and grants us a clearer vision of himself" (*CCC* 684).

In the Old Testament, God the Father is revealed. The Son and Spirit are not yet fully known. The Old Testament speaks of the Word and wisdom of God, by whom the Father creates and acts in the world, but the Word is not yet fully revealed as the beloved Son of the Father. Similarly, the Old Testament also attributes God's presence or activity in the world to the movement of his breath or spirit, but the Holy Spirit as divine person is not yet known.

In the New Testament, the Son is fully revealed by his Incarnation as man. In the life, death, and resurrection of Jesus Christ, the eternal Son of the Father is made known. The Word made flesh is revealed as the only Son of the Father, "full of grace and truth" (John 1:14). The New Testament begins to reveal the Holy Spirit. The Spirit appears descending upon Jesus. In Jesus' final discourse, preparing his disciples for his impending death and resurrection, Jesus speaks of the Spirit of Truth, whom he will send to the disciples after his glorification. "Jesus does not reveal the Holy Spirit fully, until he himself has been glorified through his death and resurrection" (*CCC* 728).

The Spirit is poured out upon the Church at Pentecost, and it is within the life of the Church where the Spirit comes to be known in a personal way. "On the day of Pentecost…Christ's Passover is fulfilled in the outpouring of the Holy Spirit, manifested, given, and communicated as a divine person.…On that day, the Holy Trinity is fully revealed" (CCC 731–732). The Father was revealed in the Old Testament. The Son was revealed in the New Testament. Saint Gregory of Nazianzus says the Spirit is known "now" within the Church, where he dwells among us. With Father and Son, the Spirit is eternal and active in creation and history from the beginning. However, the Holy Spirit is not fully known by us until he "is revealed and given, recognized and welcomed as a person" (CCC 686). This chronology of the progressive revelation of the Holy Trinity suggests that we come to know the Holy Spirit as a person as we open ourselves to his presence and activity within the Church. It is as we "welcome" the Spirit into our lives that we come to know him in a personal way.

## Divine Self-Effacement of the Holy Spirit

Understanding the progression of divine revelation, while helpful, does not remove all the difficulties that obscure our understanding of the Holy Spirit. The catechism provides a second reason for the mysterious obscurity of the Holy Spirit. The Holy Spirit does not reveal himself but is given to reveal the Father and the Son.

> Now God's Spirit, who reveals God, makes known to us Christ, his Word, his living utterance, but the Spirit does not speak of himself. The Spirit who has spoken through the prophets makes us to know the Father's Word, but we do not hear the Spirit himself (CCC 687).

When he taught about the coming Holy Spirit, Jesus said,

> When the Spirit of truth comes, he will guide you into all the truth; for he will not speak on his own, but will speak whatever he hears....He will glorify me, because he will take what is mine and declare it to you (John 16:13–14).

The Spirit makes the Son known to us and guides us into a fuller understanding of the teaching of Christ. The Son has received all things from the Father. "All that the Father has is mine" (John 16:15). The Spirit takes what belongs to the Son, which the Son has received from the Father, and declares that to us. He "declares" this truth to us, not just in words or concepts but by making us sharers in that truth, participants in the reality of new life in Christ. The Spirit enables us to share in the Son's knowledge of the Father and to enter into his prayer to the Father. "God has sent the Spirit of his Son into our hearts, crying, 'Abba! Father!'" (Galatians 4:6). *Abba*, the Aramaic word a Jew would use to address his earthly father in Jesus' day, was spoken by Jesus in prayer to his heavenly Father (Mark 14:36). That word of intimate relationship with the Father is placed upon our lips by the Holy Spirit. The Holy Spirit unites us to the Son in his prayer to the Father. The Spirit remains mysterious and hidden because he does not speak of himself but always of the Father and the Son. He does not glorify himself but glorifies the Son and, through our adoption as sons and daughters, leads us to the Father.

The Spirit is characterized by "divine self-effacement" (*CCC* 687). He does not draw our attention to himself but remains hidden and unseen as he directs us toward the Father and the Son. It is this divine self-effacement that contributes to his mystery. Because of this divine self-effacement, we cannot know the Spirit directly. We must come to know him indirectly, by the results of his activity. We come to know the Spirit, not by his own self-disclosure but by his activity through which he discloses the Father and the Son to us and makes us receptive to that disclosure through faith (*CCC* 687). We come to know the Holy Spirit by attention to the effects of his hidden presence in our midst and by welcoming him through the gifts he gives us.

## The Holy Spirit and the Revelation and Realization of Personhood

A third obstacle to our recognizing the Spirit as a person is our misunderstanding of what it means to be a person. We misinterpret the divine self-effacement of the Holy Spirit by thinking of the Spirit as something less than personal. The problem lies in our misunderstanding of what it means to be a person. We must have our understanding of personhood illuminated by divine revelation in order to grasp how fully the Holy Spirit exemplifies what it means to be a person. The meaning of personhood is revealed by Jesus Christ. Christ, by his example and teaching, shows that the true meaning of human personhood is found in the sincere gift of oneself. It is through this sincere gift of self that one finds fulfillment in communion with others. In light of Christ, we can begin to see that the divine self-effacement of the Spirit is not the negation of personhood but its full realization. The Spirit is known through his gifts because the Spirit is fully and absolutely person, fully gift, known through his total giving. The Spirit is the divine person whose personhood is revealed in total self-giving. John Paul II describes the Holy Spirit as "person-gift" (*Dominum et vivificantem* [DEV], 10). The self-giving of God to humanity is expressed by the gift of the person of the Holy Spirit. Through the Holy Spirit, God gives himself to us in a personal way. In the light of this revelation of divine personhood as gift, we come to know and understand the meaning of human personhood.

The Spirit not only reveals genuine personhood to us, the gift of the Spirit enables us to realize ourselves as persons by giving ourselves to God and others. The Spirit is given to us to enable us to realize our own human personhood. John Paul II explains how the self-opening and self-giving of God through the gift of the Holy Spirit makes possible the full realization of human personhood through self-giving. We learn from Christ the true meaning of human personhood, but we live this life of self-giving through the power of the Holy Spirit given to us by Christ. The triune God who exists as interpersonal gift in the eternal exchange of love between Father, Son, and Spirit gives himself to us through the gift of the Holy Spirit. The gift of the Spirit enables us to discover our own human personhood through the gift of our self to others (DEV 59). Through all of his many gifts, the Spirit offers himself to us so that as we receive him as a gift, we might be transformed in giving our lives as a gift back to God and in self-giving love to others. We must allow the Holy Spirit to teach us the true meaning of personhood and to help us realize our own personhood through giving. Through the divine gift of the Spirit, we are empowered to make our own lives a gift to others.

To know this divine person better and to more readily receive him as a life-transforming gift in our lives, we may begin by considering the various names by which he is known. Scripture and Tradition make use of many different names, titles, and symbols to describe the mystery of the Holy Spirit. These diverse designations reflect the many ways in which the Holy Spirit makes himself known to us. Each name, title, and symbol conveys some dimension of the mystery of the Holy Spirit and his working in our lives. By reflecting on each of these, we can grow toward a more intimate knowledge of the Spirit and a more personal relationship to him. We will begin our reflection with the simple word, "Spirit."

## Name for the Spirit

The Hebrew word for Spirit in the Old Testament is *ruah*. This word has a variety of associated meanings in Hebrew. Depending on the context, the word can mean "spirit," "wind," or "breath." Sometimes these meanings overlap. For example, the Book of Exodus describes how God makes a wind (*ruah*) blow to part the sea so the Israelites can cross to freedom (Exodus 14:21). Later, when the Israelites celebrate their deliverance in a psalm, they sing of the divine breath (*ruah*) that moved the waters aside (Exodus 15:8). The ancient Hebrews use a term from their everyday experience of nature to describe the mysterious presence of God. God's presence is like wind that moves invisibly. Like the wind, God cannot be controlled. Sometimes God moves like a mighty wind, as when he led Israel out of Egypt. Other times, God's presence is experienced like the touch of a gentle breeze. Elijah heard the voice of God in a gentle whisper (1 Kings 19:12). The Israelites also associated God's Spirit with breath, the source of life. The association between the Spirit and wind and breath continues in the New Testament. Jesus compares the Spirit to the unseen wind that blows invisibly and unpredictably (John 3:8). After his resurrection, Jesus breathes the Spirit upon the apostles, imparting the gift of new life through forgiveness of sins (John 20:22).

The New Testament uses the Greek word *pneuma* for Spirit. *Pneuma* had a general nonreligious meaning in the Greek language. It could simply mean wind, air, or gas. Our modern use of the term "pneumatic," as in pneumatic (air driven) tools, is derived from the ancient Greek usage. Some Greek philosophers used the word to describe a subtle substance suffusing and interpenetrating all things. In the Greek of the New Testament, *pneuma* begins to take on a new religious meaning. Early Christians built upon the precedence provided by the Greek translation of the Old Testament, which took this Greek term for wind and used it to translate the Hebrew word for God's Spirit. In the New Testament, the Greek word *pneuma* now designates the divine Spirit (and on occasion human or angelic spirits as well). With the adjectival form of the noun *pneumatikos*, the New Testament takes a term that could mean merely "windy" or "gaseous" in secular Greek and uses it for the adjective "spiritual" to describe the action of the Holy Spirit in the Church and in the soul. The Greek *pneuma* becomes *Spiritus* in Latin. Like Hebrew and Greek, *Spiritus* could simply mean "breath," but when used in the Latin Vulgate Bible to translate *ruah* and *pneuma*, *Spiritus* comes to refer to the divine Spirit. The adjective "spiritual" originally refers to the presence of the Holy Spirit in human experience. From that biblical vocabulary derives our modern term "spirituality." While often used today in a manner severed from these roots, the terms "spiritual" and "spirituality" originate in the New Testament experience of the Holy Spirit in the Church.

## Holy Spirit

"Holy Spirit" is the proper name of the Spirit (*CCC* 691). With the adjective "holy," the Scriptures identify the Spirit as the divine source of holiness in our lives. Only God is holy by nature. Human beings become holy by participation in God's holiness. We receive holiness as a gift from God. Mary is the model of a human being made holy by the gift of God. She teaches us how to become holy through receptivity to the Holy Spirit. We are sanctified or made holy by the Spirit. To be sanctified is to be set apart for God's possession. When we consecrate a building to serve as a church, we are sanctifying it. That building now exists completely for the service of God. God sanctifies us as his temples by sending his Spirit to dwell within us. By the indwelling Holy Spirit, our lives are given over to the service of God. When a building is sanctified to be a church, we may have to throw out some of the old furnishings and renovate the building for its new purpose. The process of sanctification by the Spirit may be likened to gradually throwing out all of the old junk in the building and filling it with those furnishings it needs to fulfill God's purpose. By the Spirit, we throw out sin and acquire new virtues. The Church Fathers speak of this sanctification as divinization. By grace we come to share in the divine life of God. The Spirit fills us with divine holiness. That holiness, which is God's by nature, becomes ours through grace (*CCC* 460, 1988, 2023–24).

The divinizing activity of the Spirit became a crucial argument for his full deity in the early Church. The Holy Spirit can only make us sharers in divine life if he himself is divine. The first Ecumenical Council of Nicea in 325 responded to the heresy of Arius (who denied the full deity of Christ) by affirming that the Son is one in being with the Father. The question of the deity of the Spirit was not addressed. The initial version of the Nicene Creed promulgated by that council simply said, "I believe in the Holy Spirit." The fuller description of the Holy Spirit as "Lord and Giver of Life, worshipped with the Father and Son" was not added until later, at the second Ecumenical Council, which met in Constantinople in 381. By that time, new heresies had risen in the Church around the question of the deity of the Holy Spirit. A group called the Macedonians denied that the Holy Spirit was fully divine. They were called Macedonians because they were followers of a bishop named Macedonius. Their opponents called them *pneumatomachians*, Greek for "Spirit fighters." When you fight against the Holy Spirit, that is not a fight you are going to win! Among the saints God raised up to oppose these "Spirit fighters" were Saint Basil the Great and his friend, Saint Gregory of Nazianzus. At the heart of Saint Gregory's argument was that the Spirit could not divinize us in baptism if he himself was not divine by nature. It is because he is holy by nature that the Spirit can make us holy by his gift of himself to us in baptism and the other sacraments. Saint Basil contrasted the uncreated Spirit who sanctifies with the created beings who are sanctified by him. He who sanctifies is divine. Those who are sanctified are created. The influence of these saints and others led the Church gathered at Constantinople to affirm the full divine nature of the Holy Spirit in an expanded Nicene Creed. The Spirit was given the divine title of "Lord." He was acknowledged as creator in the title "Giver of Life." The Spirit was acknowledged as the source of divine inspiration who spoke through the prophets. Together with the Father and the Son, the Holy Spirit receives that divine worship that is given only to God.

## Holy Ghost

In older English translations of the Bible, the Creeds, and liturgical texts, "Holy Spirit" appears as "Holy Ghost." This language persists in some of our hymns to this day. We still sing, "Come, Holy Ghost." Why was the Spirit called a "ghost?" When and how was "ghost" changed to "spirit?" The answers to these questions go back into the history of the English language. Old English, imported from its Germanic roots, reveals the word "gast" for spirit. In German, "gast" became *geist*, which remains the German word for spirit to this day. As the English language developed, "gast" became "ghost," and that is the word for spirit in such masterpieces of Elizabethan English as works of Shakespeare, the *King James Bible* of Protestants and the *Douay-Rheims Bible* used by some English-speaking Catholics. In Elizabethan English, "ghost" can refer to any sort of spirit, whether we are speaking of the Spirit of God, the human spirit or something like team spirit. The wide meaning of "ghost" is illustrated by the adjective "ghostly." In Elizabethan English, "ghostly" conveyed what we mean today by the word "spiritual." We have remnants of this older and wider use of ghost in such modern phrases as "give up the ghost" or "ghost of a chance." Since the biblical translations from Elizabethan times continued to be used all the way into the twentieth century, "Holy Ghost" remained part of our religious vocabulary long after the end of the Elizabethan era. However, the meaning of "ghost" in broader English usage changed over time. In everyday English, "ghost" lost its general meaning and now refers very specifically and almost exclusively to the spirits of deceased human beings who appear in some shadowy form among the living. When we hear the word "ghost" today, we do not think about God but rather we imagine scary apparitions appearing in haunted houses. The English language changed, and gradually religious language adjusted to this change. Beginning in the early twentieth century, modern Bible translations began to replace "Holy Ghost" with "Holy Spirit." Liturgical translations, theological works, and other religious writings gradually followed suit. Replacing "ghost" with "spirit" brought the English term closer to the Latin *Spiritus* and more accurately conveyed the meaning of the Greek and Hebrew terms. Some people mistakenly think Vatican II had something to do with the switch from "Holy Ghost" to "Holy Spirit." This change was actually under way in biblical and liturgical translations before the Second Vatican Council. However, many people only became aware of this transition after Vatican II, when they noticed "ghost" had been replaced by "spirit" in the new English translation of the Mass. We can be grateful that more accurate English translation practices have discarded this confusing use of the word "ghost" for the third person of the Trinity. However, when we encounter the "Holy Ghost" in older religious writings, we might consider it a salutary reminder that the Spirit is indeed a mysterious supernatural presence who inspires that trembling and reverential awe that the Bible calls the "fear of the Lord."

## Paraclete

Another older title for the Holy Spirit, which some modern Bible translations have replaced, is "Paraclete." This title does not go back to Old English but to the original Greek. The question translators face is whether to keep the original Greek word or to find some English equivalent. The Greek word "paraclete" is variously translated as "advocate," "defender," "comforter," "counselor," and "helper." The Spirit is given this title by Jesus in the Gospel of John (John 14:16, 26). The Holy Spirit, referred to as "another Paraclete" for Jesus, is also given this same title. Jesus is our advocate (paraclete in Greek) with the Father (1 John 2:1). Jesus intercedes for us at the right hand of the Father as our risen high priest (Romans 8:34), and the Holy Spirit intercedes for us from within our hearts in the prayers that he inspires (Romans 8:26). John Paul II emphasizes that the reference to the Spirit as "another" Paraclete shows the close communion between the work of Christ and the work of the Spirit. The Holy Spirit is called "another Paraclete" because he continues the work of Christ, the first paraclete, making us share in Christ's redeeming work (5/24/1989).

A very literal rendering of the Greek word "paraclete" could be "one called alongside to help." It was not an official title in the ancient world, but someone who came along to assist you in a trial, like a defense attorney, would be called a paraclete. The Spirit comes to assist us and help us in the various trials we face throughout life. He defends us against the attacks of evil and helps us to defend our faith when we are called upon to bear witness for Christ. The title "Paraclete" appears only in the Gospel of John, but the other Gospels describe the work of the Paraclete when they recall Jesus' promise that the Spirit would give his disciples the words to say when they are called upon to testify before their persecutors (Matthew 10:20, Mark 13:11, Luke 12:12).

## Spirit of God the Father

The Holy Spirit is referred to as the Spirit of God or the Spirit sent from God. In these passages, "God" refers primarily to the Father. Jesus promises his disciples the "Spirit of your Father" will teach you what to say when called upon to give witness to Christ (Matthew 10:20). He promises to send the Spirit who proceeds from the Father (John 15:26). Saint Peter preaches that Jesus received the Spirit from the Father and sent him to the Church on the day of Pentecost (Acts 2:33). Saint Paul says it is through Christ and in the Spirit that we have access to the Father (Ephesians 2:18) and by that Spirit that we cry out to God as our Father (Romans 8:15 and Galatians 4:6).

Both Son and Spirit have their eternal origin in the Father. The Son is eternally begotten by the Father. The Spirit eternally proceeds from the Father (and the Son). Some early Church Fathers compare this to human speech. Just as breath always accompanies our speech, so the eternal utterance of the Father's Word is eternally accompanied by the breathing forth of his Spirit. "When the Father sends his Word, he always sends his Breath. In their joint mission, the Son and the Holy Spirit are distinct but inseparable" (CCC 689). Saint Augustine tried to understand these mysteries through their image in the soul. Our soul is created in the image of God. The soul's actions of knowing and loving image the Father's eternal generation of the Son and the eternal procession of the Spirit. The generation of the Son is likened to the eternal conception of the Father's word. The Son dwells in the Father as knowledge resides in the knower. The procession of the Spirit is likened to the movement of the will in love. The Spirit is the movement of love within God. The Spirit rests in God as the beloved lies within the heart of the lover. The Son is sent into the world in the Incarnation as the Word of the Father illuminating our minds with the knowledge of God. The Spirit is sent into the world at Pentecost to inflame our hearts with the love of God.

## Spirit of Jesus Christ the Son

The Spirit who comes from the Father is also intimately related to the Son. The Spirit is both Spirit of the Father and Spirit of the Son. In the New Testament, the Spirit is variously called the Spirit of Christ, the Spirit of Jesus Christ, the Spirit of Jesus, the Spirit of the Son and the Spirit of Sonship. By the indwelling Spirit, both the Father and Son come to dwell in our hearts. The Spirit unites us to the Son and makes us sharers in his life. The Spirit fills us with the fruits of Jesus' redemptive suffering, death, and resurrection. The Son receives all things from the Father. The Spirit takes what the Son has received and imparts that to us (John 16:14–15). Saint Paul says that through the indwelling Spirit of God we have the Spirit of Christ within us (Romans 8:9–11). Through the gift of the Spirit we are united to the Son and share in his intimate relationship to the Father (Romans 8:15–16). The Holy Spirit is both Spirit of the Father and Spirit of the Son.

Both Father and Son are involved in the sending of the Spirit into the world and into our hearts. The Gospel of John says in one place that the Father will send the Spirit in Jesus' name (John 14:26). In other places, the Gospel says Jesus will send the Spirit (John 15:26 and 16:7). At the end of John's Gospel, Jesus gives the Spirit to his disciples (John 20:22). The Book of Acts describes the exalted Lord Jesus as the one who has received the Spirit from the Father and poured out the Spirit on us (Acts 2:33). According to Saint Paul, it is the Father who sends the Spirit into our hearts, but it is "the Spirit of his Son" whom the Father sends (Galatians 4:6). Taken together, these passages show that it is both Father and Son who send the Spirit.

This sending of the Spirit into the world in history reveals the procession of the Spirit within God in eternity. The mutual relationship of the Spirit to both Father and Son revealed in his gift to us shows us something about his relations to the Father and Son in the eternal life of the Trinity. To describe these relations, the Eastern Fathers of the Church often spoke of the eternal procession of the Spirit from the Father "through" the Son. Just as the Spirit of the Father is poured out to us through the Son in the history of salvation, so the Spirit proceeds from the Father through the Son in the eternal life of the Trinity. The Fathers of the Church in the Latin West often described this relation by speaking of the Spirit who proceeds from Father "and" Son. The Spirit, who is sent to us by the Father and is sent to us by the Son, must eternally proceed from both Father and Son in eternity. Eventually in the Western Latin-speaking part of the Church, the phrase "and the Son" (the single word *filioque* in Latin) was added to the Nicene Creed. In the Eastern Greek-speaking part of the Church, however, the original wording of the Creed was retained. Sadly, this difference contributed to the eventual split between the Roman Catholic Church and the Eastern Orthodox Churches beginning around the year 1000. Catholics profess the Creed with the addition of the *filioque*: the Spirit proceeds from the Father "and the Son."

The Eastern Orthodox churches preserve the original wording of the Creed: "The Spirit proceeds from the Father." Recent Catholic/Orthodox ecumenical dialogues have brought some progress in mutual understanding that raise our hopes that the *filioque* need not divide us. Despite our different versions of the Creed, our theologies are not as far apart as was once supposed. Catholic theology confesses that the Spirit proceeds from Father and Son but qualifies that confession by teaching that the Father is the eternal principle and first origin of the Spirit. Eastern Orthodox theology confesses that the Spirit proceeds from the Father but qualifies that confession by its teaching that the Spirit eternally proceeds from the Father through the Son. For this reason, the *Catechism of the Catholic Church* suggests that these differences reflect complementary rather than contradictory approaches to the mystery of the Spirit's eternal relations to Father and Son (*CCC* 247–248).

## Lord

Despite our differences over the *filioque*, Catholic and Orthodox Christians confess together that the Spirit is "the Lord, the Giver of Life." Traditional Protestants share this Nicene faith with us as well. These words were added to the Nicene Creed at the second Ecumenical Council, the Council of Constantinople, as mentioned above. With these words, the divine identity of the Holy Spirit was explicitly affirmed. The Spirit is acknowledged by the divine title of "Lord." However, the Spirit is not typically named "Lord" in Scripture. He is often referred to as the "Spirit of the Lord" but rarely "Lord." Within the New Testament, the title "Lord" usually refers to Christ the Son. However, the bishops gathered at Constantinople found a scriptural foundation for confessing the Spirit as "Lord" in Saint Paul's reference to the "Lord (who) is the Spirit" (2 Corinthians 3:17–18).

Saint Paul's designation of the Spirit as "the Lord" occurs in his spiritual interpretation of an Old Testament text from the Book of Exodus. This passage from Saint Paul not only gives us the source of this particular title for the Spirit, it also teaches us something about the work of the Spirit in our lives. Saint Paul is interpreting a passage from Exodus that recounts how Moses' face glowed when he left the presence of the Lord, so much so that he covered his face with a veil (Exodus 34:29–35). Saint Paul interprets this veil as the blindness that keeps us from recognizing Christ in the Scriptures. Saint Paul gives two sources for this veil of blindness. The devil tries to veil the truth by his lies to keep unbelievers from recognizing and responding to the glory of God revealed in the face of Jesus Christ (2 Corinthians 4:3–6). We cannot always blame the devil for our blindness, however, for we also put on our own veils that blind us to the truth. Saint Paul says that Moses put on a veil to hide the fact that the glow he had received from the presence of the Lord was fading (2 Corinthians 3:13). Saint Paul finds an analogy here of how the glory of the Old Covenant fades before the fuller glory of the New Covenant. We may find a further lesson here in the fact that Moses' veil hid his true condition. His own fading glory was hidden from others. This is the sort of veil we often wear. We hide our weakness, our sin, our need for grace from others and more importantly we try to hide these things from God. In order to see the glory of God in the face of Christ revealed in the Scriptures and to allow that glory to heal and transform us, we must remove all the veils that blind us, the veils created by the devil's lies, and our own veils with which we foolishly try to hide our true selves from God. How are these veils to be removed? As Saint Paul carefully reads the account in Exodus, he notes that when Moses turned to the Lord, the veil was removed (Exodus 34:34–35). The question to be answered in a Christian rereading and spiritual interpretation of this text from Exodus is, "Who is the 'Lord' in this passage?" Who is it that removes the veil? Saint Paul frequently applies Old Testament passages about the "Lord" to Christ the Son. On occasion, the title "Lord" designates the Father. In interpreting this specific passage, however, Saint Paul says the "Lord" is the Spirit. The "Lord" mentioned in Exodus as the one who removes the veil, is not the Lord Jesus but the Spirit of the Lord, the Holy Spirit (2 Corinthians 3:16–17). It is the Spirit who removes the veils of our blindness and allows us to see the glory of Christ with unveiled faces (2 Corinthians 3:18). This shows us that the title "Lord" can be properly attributed to the Holy Spirit and more importantly that the Spirit is the one who removes those veils that blind us to God's grace and those veils with which we blind ourselves to our own need for his grace. Through the work of the Lord who is the Spirit we are able to experience the truth of God's transforming love revealed in Christ, and by that truth, the Spirit grants us true freedom (2 Corinthians 3:17).

## Giver of Life

There are abundant references to the Spirit as the giver of life in Scripture. Jesus compares the Spirit to a river of living water (John 7:38–39), but already in the psalms the Spirit was acknowledged as the source of life. The Spirit gives life to creation and renews the earth (Psalm 104:29–30). The psalms reflect the presence of the Spirit in creation (Genesis 1:2 and 2:7). When we confess the Spirit to be the giver of life, we acknowledge a twofold gift of the Spirit. First, the Spirit is the source of all created life. By his word the Father brings creation into existence and by his Spirit he breathes life into what he has created. The Spirit is the animating principle of created life. Second, the Spirit is the source of new life, the redemptive and healing life of God poured out upon fallen creation. By the gift of the Spirit, we are created anew. The wounds of sin are healed by the gift of the Spirit. We are raised to new life in Christ (*CCC* 1988). Through the gift of the Spirit, we become part of the new creation in Christ (2 Corinthians 5:17).

## Gift and Love

The Spirit is God's first gift and the source of all other gifts (CCC 733–736). The Spirit is, above all, the gift of God's love. The love of God is poured into our hearts by the Holy Spirit, who is given to us (Romans 5:5). This gift of love is, first of all, the experience of God's love for us and, secondly, the capacity to love others with the love of God. The Spirit is given that we might know all the gifts of love that God has freely given to us (1 Corinthians 2:12). Through the gift of the Spirit we come to know the Father's love for us as his adopted and beloved children (Romans 8:14–16). The fruit of the Spirit in our lives is, above all, "love" (Galatians 5:22). This love that is poured into our hearts by the Holy Spirit has its origin in the eternal exchange of love in the Holy Trinity. After promising to send the gift of the Holy Spirit, Jesus prays to the Father that the "love with which you loved me may be in them" (John 17:26). That love with which the Father loves the Son and by which the Son returns love to the Father is the Holy Spirit. The Spirit is the eternal love between the Father and the Son. That love is poured out upon us and comes to dwell within us. We mentioned above Saint Augustine's search for an analogy to the Trinity in the human soul's actions of knowing and loving. Saint Augustine found another analogy to the Trinity in interpersonal love. In every love there is the lover, the beloved, and the love that unites them in communion. Love is a reflection of the triune God: the Father who loves, the Son who is his beloved, and the Spirit who is their love. The eternal exchange of love in the Trinity subsists as a person: the Holy Spirit. Blessed John Paul II describes the Holy Spirit as "Person-Love" and "Person-Gift" (DEV 10). The Holy Spirit is the personal expression of the divine self-giving love within the life of the Trinity given to us as love and gift. Faith is, above all, our receptivity to this gift of love, the human heart's openness to the gift of God's love given through the Holy Spirit (DEV 51).

## Gender of the Spirit

The Spirit is God, and God has no gender. "God transcends the human distinction between the sexes. He is neither man nor woman: he is God" (*CCC* 239). However, we must make use of some personal pronouns to refer to the Spirit as a divine person. We cannot reduce the Spirit to an "it." Traditionally, the Church has used masculine pronouns for the Holy Spirit. Scripture uses masculine names for the divine: God not goddess, Lord not lady. God and Lord are masculine nouns in both the Hebrew of the Old Testament (*Yahweh* and *Elohim*) and the Greek of the New Testament (*Theos* and *Kyrios*). The predominant metaphors Scripture uses to describe God, such as king, shepherd, and husband, are also masculine. While God is neither male nor female, he has adopted masculine language in his self-disclosure to us in divine revelation. In the personal self-disclosure of the Holy Trinity, God reveals his name as Father, Son, and Spirit. Father and Son naturally take masculine pronouns, and that language has been extended to the Spirit as well. In the liturgy we refer to the Spirit as "him" not "her."

Some contemporary theologians challenge this tradition and propose using feminine pronouns for the Spirit. They note that Scripture sometimes compares God's love to the love of a mother (Isaiah 49:15 and 66:13). Further, they emphasize that the Hebrew word for Spirit, *ruah*, is a feminine noun. In addition, "wisdom," which is sometimes identified with the Spirit, is a feminine noun in both Hebrew (*Hokma*) and Greek (*Sophia*). Moreover, wisdom is sometimes personified in the Old Testament as a wise woman

(Proverbs 6—8). Thus, they argue, it would make sense to refer to the Holy Spirit as "she."

Further exploration of the biblical language, however, uncovers a diversity of grammatical forms applied to the Spirit. Even within the Old Testament, the Hebrew references to the Spirit are not always consistent. While the noun *ruah* is feminine, in those few places where the full expression "Holy Spirit" appears in the Old Testament, the adjective "Holy" takes the masculine form. In the Greek translation of the Old Testament and in the New Testament, the Greek word for spirit, *pneuma*, is a neuter noun. In the Greek language, nouns can take three possible forms: masculine, feminine, or neuter. Grammatically speaking, the appropriate pronoun for *pneuma* is neither "he" nor "she" but "it." Of course, that does not mean the Spirit is an "it," an impersonal force. We must remember that grammatical gender, whether masculine, feminine, or neuter does not always signify whether something is male, female, personal, or impersonal. To say that a noun is grammatically feminine, masculine, or neuter is simply to identify the sort of ending or form that noun takes. Moreover, in the Gospel of John, we see a shift from the neuter to the masculine pronoun for the Spirit. In the Gospel of John, Jesus names the Holy Spirit with the masculine noun Paraclete. Paraclete takes the masculine pronoun "he." In this way, John emphasizes that the Spirit is revealed as a person. While the original word for spirit in the Hebrew is feminine and the original word in Greek is neuter, in both Testaments we see a movement toward masculine language when the personhood of the Spirit is emphasized. When we get glimpses of the Spirit's full personal name (Holy Spirit) in the Old Testament, the feminine noun is modified by a masculine adjective. In the New Testament, when Jesus most fully discloses the Spirit as a person, the Spirit is named by the masculine noun Paraclete. There is a similar shift in the New Testament away from the feminine nouns and images used for wisdom in the Old Testament. In the New Testament wisdom is linked to the masculine noun Word (*Logos*). Jesus, the Son, is identified as the Incarnation of wisdom.

The modern proposal to use feminine pronouns for the Spirit runs the danger of dividing the Spirit from the Father and the Son. Using feminine language to describe one person of the Trinity introduces sexual differentiation and division into God. In the history of religions, goddess language is invariably polytheistic, occurring where there are many gods and goddesses. The Holy Trinity is one God and must not be misunderstood as a collection of two gods and a goddess. In the divine activity of creating and redeeming, God is one. Father, Son, and Spirit act as one principle of action in every divine activity. "Inseparable in what they are, the divine persons are also inseparable in what they do" (*CCC* 267). The actions of Father, Son, and Spirit cannot be differentiated or divided into masculine and feminine activities. As the Spirit of the Father and the Son, the Holy Spirit shares in their relationship to creation and God's people. It is the nature of that relationship between God and his people that is conveyed by the masculine language of Scripture and Tradition.

This biblical preference for masculine language for God does not mean that God is male but rather describes God's relationship to us. His love is the gratuitous love of a merciful Father who freely chooses to embrace us and adopt us as his beloved children (Deuteronomy 32:6, Isaiah 63:13, and 1 John 3:1). More significantly, God's love is also a spousal love toward his people as his bride (Isaiah 54:5, Jeremiah 2:2, Ezekiel 16:8, and Hosea 2:19). Through the redemptive spousal love of God, we are invited to union with him by responding to his divine self-communication. The spousal love of God is embodied in Jesus Christ, the divine bridegroom who gives himself to his beloved bride in faithful and fruitful love (Ephesians 5:25, 32). God is the divine bridegroom who initiates a relationship with us. The Church, or the soul, is the bride who responds to his gift. The Spirit is the gift of divine spousal love poured into our hearts.

## The Spirit as Spouse of the Blessed Virgin Mary

The Spirit's relationship to us as spousal love is most clearly revealed by his relationship to the Blessed Virgin Mary. One of John Paul II's general audiences on the Holy Spirit focuses on the Blessed Virgin Mary as the spouse of the Holy Spirit (5/2/1990). John Paul II begins with the prophetic expressions of God's eternal love for his people, the "virgin Israel" returning from exile to her loving God (Jeremiah 31:4), the once forsaken and grieved wife now embraced by God her "husband...and redeemer" (Isaiah 54:5–8); the adulterous wife who has been forgiven and embraced by the steadfast love of God (Hosea 2:21–22). These prophecies portray God's love for his people Israel (who represents humanity) as an eternal spousal love that is greater than human sin. These prophecies find their fulfillment in a manner exceeding all human expectations: in the Incarnation. This spousal love of God is expressed by the person of the Holy Spirit. The Spirit is revealed, says John Paul II, as "God the Spouse." In this fulfillment, Mary represents the Virgin-Israel from the prophecy of Jeremiah. Mary expresses the perfect "yes" of the bride to the spousal love of God. The gift of the Spirit to Mary and her response express the supreme union of love between God and humanity. This is why Mary is called "spouse of the Holy Spirit." As spouse of the Holy Spirit, Mary models for us how we should respond to the Spirit in faith, love, and obedience. John Paul II presents Mary as the type or symbol, the model and example of the spousal union with the Holy Spirit that is offered to each one of us.

John Paul II credits Saint Francis of Assisi for introducing this Marian title into the vocabulary of the Church. While he is no doubt correct that the title was popularized by the influence of Saint Francis, it can be found as far back as the eighth century. Modern saints who have emphasized Mary's role as spouse of the Spirit include Saint Louis de Montfort (whose Marian spirituality had a decisive influence on John Paul II) and Saint Maximilian Kolbe (whom John Paul II canonized). The title appears in the writings of Popes Leo XIII, Pius XII, and Paul VI, as well as John Paul II's own encyclical on the Blessed Virgin Mary (*Redemptoris Mater*, 26).

Mary bears the spiritual fruit of holiness and thus teaches us the way to spiritual fruitfulness through receptivity to the Holy Spirit. Her spousal union with the Spirit also bears fruit in maternity. The bride becomes mother, first of all, of Jesus Christ, God incarnate. Then, as the fruit of her lifelong faithful spousal love, she is given to us as our mother. The proposal to use feminine language for the Spirit expresses a genuine spiritual need. There is a need to experience God's love in a maternal and feminine form. However, God has foreseen and met that need. We do not need to change the Spirit into a mother by changing the traditional language of the Church. The Spirit has provided us with a mother. The Blessed Virgin Mary, spouse of the Spirit, was especially graced and guided by the Spirit to fulfill her vocation. The Spirit formed her first of all to become the mother of God in the Incarnation of the Son and then to become, at the cross, the mother of the Church (John 19:26–27). Rather than changing the traditional language of the Church to portray the Spirit as mother, we ought rather to receive the one who has been especially graced by the Spirit to be our mother. In the Blessed Virgin Mary, the love of God is given to us in a genuinely human, feminine, and maternal way. By her example and by her intercessions, Mary, the spouse of the Spirit and our mother, teaches us the way of spiritual fruitfulness through receptivity to the gift of the Spirit.

## Symbols of the Spirit

The mystery of the Spirit and his working is not exhausted by these names and titles given to him by Scripture and Tradition. While it must be emphasized that the Spirit is a divine person, we must also not lose sight that this divine person is quite mysterious. The Spirit is personal but far transcends the limitations of a human person. The ancient words used for "Spirit" already link the Holy Spirit to such natural symbols as wind and breath. When the Spirit appears, he does not take human form like the incarnate Son but appears as a dove or as fire. Other symbols are reflected in the sacramental practices of the Church. The catechism lists the following symbols of the Spirit: water, anointing with oil, fire, cloud and light, seal, laying on of hands, finger, and dove (*CCC* 694–701). We will explore the meaning of each of these symbols to further reflect on the mystery of the Holy Spirit.

## Wind

Jesus uses the analogy of wind to describe this mystery of the Holy Spirit (John 3:1–8). The Gospel of John relates how Nicodemus, a member of the ruling body of the Jews in Jerusalem (the Sanhedrin), comes secretly to Jesus in the night to learn from him. Jesus immediately challenges this teacher to recognize the limits of his understanding, telling him that he must be born anew of the

Spirit if he wishes to understand the kingdom of God. Nicodemus replies with puzzlement, trying to understand Jesus' words within the framework of natural birth. "Can one enter a second time into the mother's womb and be born," he asks (John 3:4)? Nicodemus does not grasp that Jesus is speaking of a rebirth in the Holy Spirit. He tries to interpret Jesus' words in terms of what can be seen, but the Spirit is unseen. Jesus helps Nicodemus by comparing the Holy Spirit to the wind, which "blows where it chooses, and you hear the sound of it, but you do not know where it comes from or where it goes" (John 3:8).

By this analogy, Jesus points to the mystery of the Holy Spirit, who, like the wind, moves invisibly and often unpredictably. When the wind blows, you do not see the wind itself but you see the effects of its movement. You see the branches move this way and that. You may feel the gentle touch of the wind in a slight breeze. You may see an entire landscape transformed by the power of the wind blowing in a storm. You see the operation and effects of the wind, but the wind itself remains invisible. All of these aspects of wind make it an apt analogy for the movement of the Spirit. We do not see the Spirit himself, but we may observe the effects of his movement. We come to know the Spirit by giving our attention to the effects of his presence moving in the Church and in our souls. As we open ourselves to the wind of the Spirit, we can come to know him by welcoming his presence in our lives.

## Breath

In Genesis, God breathes on Adam, and he becomes a living soul (Genesis 2:7). In the Gospel of John, Jesus breathes on the apostles, imparting the new life that comes from the forgiveness of sins (John 20:21–23). The language of breath points to the life-giving power of the Spirit. The symbolism of breath also points to the Spirit's divine origin. Proceeding from God, the Spirit is the communication of divine life. The Spirit comes from the life of God and brings life to God's creation. Breath has the power to raise someone from impending death, as when a lifeguard breathes life into someone he has rescued from drowning. Jesus saves us from sin and death and breathes new life into us through the Holy Spirit. The breath of God raises us from spiritual death and fills us with divine life.

## Water

The Spirit is a "river of living water" (John 7:38–39). The Spirit is "poured out" upon us like rain (Acts 2:33). The Spirit "fills us" like a liquid and even intoxicates us like wine (Ephesians 5:18). This language conveys the Spirit's capacity to penetrate and permeate the human being with his presence. Conversely, this language implies the human capacity to receive and to be filled by this divine presence. This water language expresses the divinizing activity of the Spirit and the human receptivity to that divine action. As described by Saint Athanasius, "By the participation of the Spirit, we become communicants in the divine nature....For this reason, those in whom the Spirit dwells are divinized" (CCC 1988). In the light of this "water" language of the Spirit, we may compare human nature to a sponge. Just as a sponge has the capacity to receive and be permeated by water, so human nature has the capacity to receive and be permeated by God. Just as that sponge has to be squeezed out in order to receive fresh water, so we must empty ourselves in order to be filled with God. The "liquidity" of the Spirit conveyed by the symbolism of water expresses the Spirit's ability to permeate and fill us with divine life. As we are filled and permeated by the Spirit, we will come to understand this water language in another way. The Spirit is that living water that alone can quench our spiritual thirst (John 4:14). So satisfying is that living water, it may be compared to wine, the new wine of grace which abundantly quenches the human thirst for God (John 2:10 and Mark 2:22).

## Anointing With Oil

The presence of the Spirit is symbolized by the anointing with oil. Those baptized receive the oil of chrism. This signifies our share in Jesus' anointing by the Holy Spirit at his baptism. Anointed by the Spirit, we share in the prophetic, priestly, and kingly mission of Jesus (*CCC* 1241). At confirmation, we are anointed with oil as a sign of our consecration to Christ and the infilling of the Spirit through which our lives will give off the "aroma of Christ" (*CCC* 1294). In the anointing of the sick, the oil signifies the healing presence of the Spirit (*CCC* 1520). Those who are ordained to the priesthood receive the anointing of oil to signify the gift of the Spirit who will make their ministry fruitful (*CCC* 1574). The use of oil in these sacraments is rooted in the ancient uses of oil in biblical times:

> Oil is a sign of abundance and joy, it cleanses (anointing before and after a bath) and limbers (the anointing of athletes); oil is a sign of healing, since it is soothing to bruises and wounds; and it makes one radiant with beauty, health, and strength (*CCC* 1293).

Like the ancient practices of anointing with oil, the Holy Spirit coming to rest upon us brings cleansing, strength, healing, and joy.

## Fire

The Holy Spirit appeared at Pentecost as tongues of fire resting upon each apostle. The fire of the Holy Spirit is a purifying fire. Like gold that is purified in a furnace, so the impurities of our soul are burned away by the fiery love of the Spirit. The fire is also a sign of the divine nature of the Spirit. God's presence was manifested in the Old Testament by the burning bush. God descended upon Mount Sinai in fire (Exodus 3:2 and 19:18). The New Testament declares that "our God is a consuming fire" (Hebrews 12:29). The fire of Pentecost is a visible manifestation that this Spirit is indeed God, who is coming to dwell in his people. The fire of God within the soul is not always a blazing furnace of purification. Fire also symbolizes the gentle flame of the Spirit that warms cold hearts. In the traditional prayer to the Creator Spirit, *Veni Creator Spiritus*, we ask the Spirit to inflame our hearts with love. In the sequence of the Holy Spirit, *Veni Sancte Spiritus*, we ask the Spirit to fill the frozen heart with fervor. Through these prayers, the Church teaches us to pray that the fire of the Spirit continues to burn in our hearts lest we grow cold in our love.

## Cloud and Light

In the Old Testament, God appeared in a bright cloud of glory (*CCC* 697). This cloud descended upon Mount Sinai when the Law was given (Exodus 24:15–18). The cloud led Israel through the wilderness and came to rest upon the tabernacle tent when they camped (Exodus 33:9–10 and 40:36–38). When the temple of Solomon was dedicated, the cloud filled the building with such brightness that the priests could not minister (1 Kings 8:9–10). In Jewish tradition, this visible manifestation of divine glory was called *Shekinah*. The *Shekinah* was God's presence dwelling with God's people. The *Shekinah* appears in the New Testament as the cloud that envelops Jesus and his three disciples on the mount of transfiguration (Luke 9:34–35). At the ascension, Jesus disappears into this cloud of glory, and it is upon that cloud that he will appear again at his Second Coming (Acts 1:9 and Luke 21:27). These visible manifestations of divine glory are reflections of the person of the Holy Spirit, who manifests and glorifies the Father and the Son. Like the cloud that accompanied and led Israel through her wilderness wanderings, so the Spirit accompanies and guides the Church on her pilgrimage through history to meet the Lord at his coming.

## Seal

The seal in antiquity was a mark of ownership stamped or imprinted on an object or tattooed on a soldier or slave. The seal of the Holy Spirit is the invisible imprint of the Spirit upon our soul that marks us as God's property. "This seal of the Holy Spirit marks our total belonging to Christ, our enrollment in his service for ever as well as the promise of divine protection" (*CCC* 1296). The Spirit is God's gift to mark us as his own beloved. It is the mark of our consecration as his priestly people. The seal of the Spirit is also God's pledge to make good on his claim of ownership over our lives, to complete the work of redemption that he has begun in us, and to bring us to eternal life with him in heaven (2 Corinthians 1:22, Ephesians 1:13, and 4:30).

## Laying on of Hands

Beginning with the apostles, the Spirit is given through the laying on of hands. As successors to the apostles, the bishops impart the Holy Spirit through the laying on of hands in confirmation and in the ordination of priests (*CCC* 1288, 1573). In this laying on of hands we see how the gift of the Spirit has been personally handed on from Jesus to his apostles, from the apostles to their successors the bishops, from the bishops to priests, to each baptized and confirmed Catholic to this very day. We enter into communion with the Spirit in and through our communion with the Church. This is illustrated by the early history of the Church recorded in the Book of Acts. When the people of Samaria were converted to the Gospel, the Apostles John and Peter were sent to lay hands on them to receive the Spirit (Acts 8:14–17). This signified to all that the Samaritans had received the same Spirit who was poured out upon the apostles at Pentecost and that they were incorporated into the one apostolic community founded by Christ. This does not mean that the sovereign movement of the Spirit is restricted. For instance, when Peter went to preach to the gentiles gathered at the house of Cornelius, while he was still preaching, before Peter could lay hands on any of them, the Spirit was poured out. These gentiles began praising God in tongues just as the apostles did on Pentecost. Yet the importance of communion with the Church was illustrated by Peter's insistence that these gentiles be immediately baptized (Acts 10:44–48). The movement of the Spirit cannot be restricted to the sacraments. An authentic movement of the Spirit, however, leads toward sacramental communion with the apostolic community. The laying on of hands links us to one another in this community founded upon the apostles and perpetuated through their successors. This is a sign that our communion with the Holy Spirit is a communion with one another in the Church. This communion with one another in the Holy Spirit is a sign and reflection of the communion of the Holy Trinity.

By the laying on of hands in confirmation, we are also sent into the world to be agents of the Spirit's work of communion. The Spirit leads us first of all toward unity in charity within the Catholic Church (*CCC* 813). The Spirit also inspires movements to heal the wounds to unity caused by divisions in the past, leading us to work toward the reunion of all Christians (*CCC* 820). Moreover, through the Holy Spirit, the Church is to be a sacramental sign and instrument of the unity of the human race (*CCC* 774–776).

## Finger of God

In the Gospel of Matthew, Jesus says, "If it is by the Spirit of God that I cast out demons, then the kingdom of God has come to you" (Matthew 12:28). In the parallel passage in Luke, Jesus says, "If it is by the finger of God that I cast out the demons, then the kingdom of God has come to you" (Luke 11:20). Thus, the Gospel accounts equate the Spirit with the finger of God. The *Veni Creator Spiritus* prayer calls the Spirit the "finger of the Father's right hand." This language describes the Spirit as the touch of God. When we experience the touch of God, we experience the Holy Spirit. It could be a touch that drives out demons and brings deliverance from evil, a sign of the coming of God's kingdom. It could be the touch of God that brings healing. It could be the touch of God that grants strength to endure sickness when there is no physical healing. It might be the touch of God that imparts a word of wisdom in answer to a prayer for guidance. It will often be that touch that makes us aware and conscious of the Lord's presence in our prayer, in the liturgy, or in the midst of a busy day. In each of these moments where we are somehow touched by God, we are experiencing the presence of the Holy Spirit in our lives. That touch from God that warns us when we are tempted to sin is the Holy Spirit. That touch from God that keeps us from sin is the Holy Spirit. On the other hand, that touch from God that calls us to repentance and leads us to confession after we sin is also the Holy Spirit. We may recognize the touch of the Spirit for he is always full of mercy and love. This divine finger always points us toward Christ and directs us in the path of holiness. As we grow in intimacy with the Spirit, we will become ever more sensitive and docile to his divine touch.

## Dove

We will conclude our reflections on the names, titles, and symbols of the Holy Spirit by considering the beautiful form in which the Spirit appeared as he descended upon Jesus at his baptism: the dove. The descent of the Spirit in the form of a dove appears in all four Gospels (Matthew 3:16, Mark 1:10, Luke 3:22, and John 1:32). A dove appears in the Old Testament to Noah as the flood recedes and the ark approaches land. The presence of the dove is a sign to Noah announcing the end of the divine judgment upon the earth and the dawning of a new world. The Holy Spirit takes the form of a dove descending upon Jesus to announce the end of the flood of sin and death that threatened to drown humanity. The descent of the Holy Spirit announces the dawning of a new world through the death and resurrection of Christ that his baptism foreshadows. The visible descent of the Spirit is also a sign for us, to show us what happens invisibly in our own baptism. The Spirit descends to fill us with the gift of peace through baptism. Through the forgiveness of sins, we are at peace with God, and through the power of the indwelling Spirit we may become agents of peace in this world. The Church Fathers noted many ways in which the dove was a suitable symbol for the Spirit. The dove is a peaceful bird that eats the seeds and fruit of the earth, unlike birds of prey, which kill for their food. Doves are not solitary birds but enjoy the company of other doves. Doves like to nest in and near human dwellings, just as the Spirit desires to dwell in humanity. Doves appear to kiss one another with their beaks when they are perched side by side. In this the dove reflects the love of the Holy Spirit. The soft cooing of doves is compared to the gentle sighs and groans of prayer that the Spirit inspires within us (Romans 8:23, 26). In all of these ways, the symbol of the dove shows the charity, peace, and gentleness of the Spirit and the fruits that the Spirit seeks to impart to the Church. The Church is called to imitate the Holy Spirit, since she, too, is called a dove. In the divine bridegroom's song to the Church as his beloved bride, he calls the Church his dove (Song of Songs 6:9).

## REFLECTION QUESTIONS

1.  *Why is the Spirit so mysterious to us?*

2.  *Which names of the Spirit express most clearly his divine nature?*

3.  *What do the Spirit's names and titles reveal about his presence and work in our lives?*

4.  *How is the Holy Spirit related to the Father and to the Son? How are east and west both similar and different in their understanding of the Spirit's relation to the Son?*

5.  *What is the significance of anointing with oil and laying on of hands in the Church's sacramental practice? How have you experienced the presence of the Spirit when receiving or observing the anointing and laying on of hands?*

6.  *Which of the symbols of the Spirit best reflect your experience of the Spirit? Have you experienced the Spirit as a purifying fire? As the touch of God's finger? As the water of life?*

# CHAPTER 2

# The History of the Spirit Through Sacred Scripture

## *The Holy Spirit in the Bible*

While the person of the Spirit was not fully disclosed until Pentecost, the history of the Holy Spirit can be traced in the Scriptures from creation forward through the Old Testament, reaching fulfillment in the New Testament. The Spirit was present and active in the creation of the world. His power is manifested in the history of Israel. The prophets of Israel foretell the Spirit's anointing of the Messiah and his future outpouring upon all humanity. In the New Testament, the promises of the Spirit-anointed Messiah find their fulfillment with the coming of Christ. The Spirit is present in the life of Jesus from the annunciation to the resurrection. The Old Testament promises of the universal gift of the Spirit are fulfilled by his outpouring on the day of Pentecost. The presence and activity of the Holy Spirit pervade the history of the early Church in the Book of Acts, and he is frequently mentioned in the letters of the New Testament. In this chapter, we trace this history of the Spirit with an overview of the biblical teaching on the Spirit from Genesis to the Book of Revelation.

## Promise of the Spirit in the Old Testament

In the Old Testament, "two prophetic lines were to develop, one leading to the expectation of the Messiah, the other pointing to the announcement of a new Spirit" (*CCC* 711). Many of us are familiar with that first line of development, the prophecies of the coming Messiah and their fulfillment by Christ. Many are less familiar with the parallel development in which the Old Testament prophetically prepares for the coming gift of the Holy Spirit. Both the coming of Christ and the coming of the Holy Spirit are prefigured and foreshadowed in the Old Testament.

The Old Testament does not reveal the Holy Spirit in his fullness as a divine person, but it does speak of the divine activity in the world as the presence of God's breath or Spirit. Spirit, in the Old Testament, designates the mode of God's presence and activity in the world. God breathes his Spirit into creation and history to accomplish his will. This movement of the Spirit will continue in the New Testament, where the divine breath will be revealed as a divine person promised by the Father and given to us by the Son.

## The Holy Spirit in Creation

The Holy Spirit appears in the opening verses of Scripture, although not as explicitly in some modern Bible translations as others. Genesis opens with the words, "In the beginning when God created the heavens and the earth…the Spirit of God swept over the face of the waters" (Genesis 1:1–2, as translated in an NRSV footnote). Modern English translations of the Bible vary in how they translate the Hebrew words *ruah* (spirit, breath, or wind) and *Elohim* (of God). The phrase in Genesis 1:2 appears variously as "Spirit of God" or "wind from God" or "mighty wind (treating *Elohim* as an adjective, as in "God-like" or "mighty"). Since this passage describes the divine activity of creation, the traditional translation of "Spirit of God" best conveys the sense of the passage. This is no natural wind but the divine presence that brings life to that which God has called into existence by his word. The second chapter of Genesis says God breathed into man the breath of life, and man became a living being (Genesis 2:7). That wind that moved over the newly created world is the Spirit that God breathes into the world to give it life. When God restores creation after the flood, once again this divine wind or Spirit moves over the water to bring forth life (Genesis 8:1).

This reading of Genesis is confirmed by later passages of the Old Testament that associated the divine Spirit or breath with creation. God creates both by his creative spoken word, "Let there be light!" and also by his life-giving breath. The psalms praise the Creator with the words, "By the word of the LORD the heavens were made, and all their hosts by the breath of his mouth" (Psalm 33:6). Judith likewise praises God the Creator in similar words, "Let all your creatures serve you, for you spoke, and they were made. You sent forth your spirit, and it formed them" (Judith 16:14). The Spirit of God is the source of life. "When you send forth your spirit, they are created; and you renew the face of the ground" (Psalm 104:30). The Father creates by his word and breath, the Son and Spirit (*CCC* 290–292, 703). The Creed affirms the role of each person of the Trinity in creation when it refers to the Father as "maker of heaven and earth" and says of the Son that "through him all things were made" and calls the Spirit, "the giver of life."

In the New Testament, the Spirit appears as the source of life in the new creation. The Spirit is "the giver of life" in two senses. The Spirit is the source of original created life and also the source of the new life in Christ. Created good by God, but wounded by sin, creation itself groans for redemption, a groaning that the Spirit himself prays through us (Romans 8:19–26). God, who created the world by his word and breath, restores creation by the Word incarnate, who breathes his life-giving Spirit to bring forgiveness of sins and healing (John 20:22). In Saint John's heavenly vision of the "new heavens and earth," the Spirit, symbolically portrayed as the "river of the water of life," will bring healing to the nations (Revelation 22:1–2).

## Empowering of the Spirit in the Old Testament

In the Old Testament, God saves his people by empowering leaders with his Spirit. The Spirit describes the presence of God anointing his chosen leaders with divine power. The Spirit was upon Moses (Numbers 11:17). His successor, Joshua, "was full of the spirit of wisdom, because Moses had laid his hands on him" (Deuteronomy 34:9; see also Numbers 27:18). Several times in the Book of Judges, we read how the Spirit of the Lord came upon Gideon, Jephthah, Samson, and other judges to strengthen them so they could liberate the Israelites from their oppressors (Judges 3:10, 6:34, 11:29, and 14:6, 19). Even though these leaders were often weak and their armies small, God gave them victory over their enemies. Those victories confirm the Lord's words, "Not by might, nor by power, but by my spirit, says the LORD of hosts" (Zechariah 4:6). Salvation comes not by human strength but by God's power working through his chosen human instruments. When Samuel anointed David as God's chosen king for Israel, "the Spirit of the LORD came mightily upon David from that day forward" (1 Samuel 16:13). At the end of his life, David declares, "the Spirit of the LORD speaks through me" (2 Samuel 23:2). In addition to Israel's leaders, the Spirit is also given to Israel's prophets. The prophet Hosea is called a "man of the spirit" (Hosea 9:7). Micah is "filled with power, with the spirit of the LORD" (Micah 3:8). It is by his Spirit that the Lord speaks to his people through the prophets (Nehemiah 9:30 and Zechariah 7:12). All of these Spirit-anointed leaders and prophets in the history of Israel foreshadow the coming Messiah upon whom the Spirit of the Lord will rest (Isaiah 11:2 and 61:1). Jesus begins his public ministry by proclaiming himself as the one foretold by Isaiah, saying, "The Spirit of the Lord is upon me, because he has anointed me to bring good news....Today this scripture has been fulfilled" (Luke 4:17–21).

Not only does the Old Testament speak of the great anointing of the Spirit that will belong to the Messiah, it also speaks of a universal outpouring of the Spirit upon all God's people in the messianic age. The Spirit, who was given only to particular chosen leaders and prophets in the Old Testament, will be given to all in the New Covenant. This future universal outpouring of the Spirit and his gifts is first indicated when the Spirit given to Moses is shared with the seventy elders of Israel (Numbers 11:16–30). Moses is overburdened with the tasks of leadership, and the Lord responds to his need by coming down upon the tabernacle in a cloud, a visible manifestation of his glory, and then taking the Spirit from Moses and distributing it to the seventy elders. As the Spirit falls upon them, all the elders begin to prophesy. Two of these elders were not gathered with the others in the tabernacle, and yet the Spirit comes upon them and they prophesy as well. Joshua was offended by these elders prophesying outside of the place of worship, but Moses replied, "Would that all the LORD's people were prophets, and that the LORD would put his spirit on them" (Numbers 11:29)!

Moses' desire for a universal outpouring of the Spirit finds its answer in the divine promise spoken through the prophets. Through Isaiah, the Lord promises to pour out the Spirit upon all the offspring and descendents of his people (Isaiah 44:3). Through the prophet Joel, God says, "I will pour out my spirit on all flesh; your sons and your daughters shall prophesy, your old men shall dream dreams, your young men shall see visions. Even on the male and female slaves, in those days, I will pour out my spirit" (Joel 2:28–29). Joel says the day will come when the Spirit will be poured out on all God's people, young and old, male and female, master and servant, and they will receive divine communication in the form of prophecies, dreams, and visions. On the day of Pentecost, Saint Peter cites this prophesy of Joel and declares to those looking on that this outpouring of the Spirit that they "both see and hear" is the fulfillment of "what was spoken through the prophet Joel." Then Peter invites them to be baptized and receive the gift of the Holy Spirit (Acts 2:16, 33, 38).

## The Spirit of Wisdom in the Old Testament

In the Old Testament, the Spirit is sometimes associated with wisdom. The skill of the Israelite artisan named Bezalel, who is called upon to produce the tent of worship and all its sacred furnishings, is attributed to the Spirit (Exodus 31:3). The Book of Job says it is "the breath of the Almighty" who gives understanding (Job 32:8). The fullest depiction of the Spirit as wisdom is found in the Wisdom of Solomon. Wisdom is a kindly spirit that both fills the world and dwells in the soul that receives her discipline (Wisdom 1:5–7). In the seventh chapter of this book, wisdom is described as a spirit who is intelligent, holy, all-powerful, all-seeing, penetrating, and pervading all things. Wisdom is an emanation from God, who dwells with holy souls, making them friends of God and prophets (Wisdom 7:22–27). The Spirit is divine wisdom dwelling in receptive souls. This Old Testament wisdom tradition finds its fulfillment in the New Testament. In the Gospel of John, Jesus, the Incarnation of wisdom, promises to send the Spirit of truth to dwell in his followers, teaching them all things (John 16:13). Saint Paul speaks of the wisdom given to us by the Spirit of God, who reveals "the depths of God" to those who have received him (1 Corinthians 2:10–14). Through the gift of the Spirit we receive the "mind of Christ" (1 Corinthians 2:16).

## The Old Testament Promise of the Spirit of Holiness

The prophetic promises of the coming messianic age and the new covenant that God will make with his people focus on the gift of the indwelling Spirit. By this indwelling, the people will be sanctified, made holy, and consecrated to God as his own people. Jeremiah introduces the promises of the new covenant, saying, "The days are surely coming, says the LORD, when I will make a new covenant with the house of Israel and the house of Judah….I will put my law within them, and I will write it on their hearts; and I will be their God, and they shall be my people" (Jeremiah 31:31, 33). The prophet Ezekiel develops this theme further with the explanation that the law will be written upon hearts transformed by the indwelling Spirit. "A new heart I will give you, and a new Spirit I will put within you….I will put my Spirit within you, and make you follow my statutes…. You shall by my people, and I will be your God" (Ezekiel 36:26–28). These promises of the new covenant are fulfilled by the coming of the Spirit to dwell in the Church as a temple (1 Corinthians 3:16–

17). In this new covenant, God promises to dwell within his people, making us holy by his indwelling presence. By the indwelling Holy Spirit, we are brought into communion with the Holy Trinity that we might become the holy temple, the dwelling place of God.

Ezekiel also speaks of this new covenant as the restoration and resurrection of the people of God. The prophet is taken in a vision to a valley filled with bones and told to prophesy over the bones. As he prophesies, the Spirit restores flesh to the bones and raises them to life. The Lord then says to Ezekiel, "I will put my Spirit within you, and you shall live" (Ezekiel 37:14). This finds fulfillment in the New Testament witness to the Spirit as the power of resurrection life. Saint John speaks of the life-giving qualities of the Spirit (John 7:38), and Saint Paul associates the Spirit with resurrection life and the future redemption of the body (Romans 8:11).

## The Departure of the Spirit and the Desire for His Return

The latter parts of the Book of Isaiah reflect the perspective of the Israelites in exile, still suffering for their sins and longing for the restoration of the divine presence in their midst. Isaiah laments the departure of the presence of the "Holy Spirit." This is one of the very few references in the Old Testament to "Holy Spirit" rather than simply "Spirit" or "Spirit of God." This title, which appears twice in this lament, conveys something of a divine personal presence. In these passages, the Old Testament comes closest to the New Testament revelation of the Spirit as a person. The lament begins by recalling that it was no messenger or angel but God himself who saved Israel from Egyptian slavery. It was the Holy Spirit, who was in their midst, who rescued them and guided them. Yet, they grieved the Holy Spirit by their sin and now long for his presence (Isaiah 63:10–

14). A similar lament appears on a more individual and personal level in Psalm 51, a penitential psalm known in Catholic tradition as the *Miserere*. The psalmist confesses his sin and begs the Lord, "Do not cast me away from your presence, and do not take your holy spirit from me" (Psalm 51:11). The Old Testament witnesses to the painful absence of the Spirit due to our sin and gives voice to penitential prayer for his return. Responding to that desire for the return of the Spirit, the prophet Zechariah promises the Israelites, who have returned from exile, that the Lord will come again to dwell with them, gathering many other nations into the people of God as well. The Lord will pour out his Spirit as a spirit of grace and supplication and a fountain to purify from sin (Zechariah 12:10 and 13:1).

Zechariah was one of the last prophets to speak to Israel. The voice of prophecy ceases in Israel not long after their return from exile (1 Maccabees 9:27). Many Israelites saw this disappearance of prophecy as a manifestation of the absence of the Holy Spirit in their midst. The voice of the Spirit was no longer heard in the land. Hence it is no surprise that when a prophet finally appeared in the wilderness baptizing repentant sinners in the Jordan river, "people from the whole Judean countryside and all the people of Jerusalem were going out to him" (Mark 1:5). Those who came to see John the Baptist heard him proclaim that he was preparing the way for one who would baptize in the Holy Spirit. The faithful who awaited the coming Messiah and longed for the promised outpouring of the Spirit gathered to see if the time for fulfillment had indeed arrived. Among the faithful ones of Israel, however, there was one, a young woman, who had already been overshadowed by the Spirit and had welcomed the coming of the Messiah.

## Mary Receives the Spirit and Foreshadows Pentecost

Mary's entire life is marked by the action of the Holy Spirit. The angel Gabriel's greeting to her, "Hail Mary, full of grace," acknowledged the fullness of grace that the Spirit gave Mary from the moment of her conception. By her response to this annunciation, by her total "yes," Mary became both temple and spouse of the Holy Spirit. The Spirit overshadowed her, and the child Jesus was conceived in her womb by the Spirit (Matthew 1:20 and Luke 1:35). John Paul II points to Mary's response to the Spirit as a shining model for each of us to emulate in our personal relationship to God. Mary represents the perfect response of created love to the uncreated divine love of the Holy Spirit. We, too, are called to respond to the love of God with our own "yes" to the Holy Spirit (4/18/1990).

The gift of the Spirit to Mary foreshadows his coming to the Church at Pentecost. Luke begins his Gospel with the annunciation to Mary. Mary also appears at the beginning of Luke's history of the Church in the Book of Acts—Mary is there in the upper room with the apostles praying for the coming of the Spirit (Acts 1:14). Thus, Luke's two-volume work links Mary both to the birth of the Messiah and to the birth of the Church. The two events are further linked by Saint Luke's description of the common effects of the coming of the Spirit upon Mary and the Church. As a result of the coming of the Holy Spirit upon the Church at Pentecost, the disciples are "filled" with the Holy Spirit, and they begin to rejoice and magnify God. The gift of prophecy is poured out by the Spirit (Acts 2:11, 17).

These same results are foreshadowed by the coming of the Spirit at the annunciation to Mary. Mary and those around her are filled with the Spirit and begin to magnify God in prophetic speech. After the Spirit overshadows Mary, she soon visits Elizabeth, who is "filled with the Spirit" and begins to prophesy, "Blessed are you among women, and blessed is the fruit of your womb" (Luke 1:42)! Not only that, the baby in Elizabeth's womb, John the Baptist, leaps for joy, a sign that he, too, was filled with the Spirit while still in his mother's womb (Luke 1:15, 41). Mary herself responds by magnifying God, praising him for the great things he has done in her beautiful inspired prayer, the Magnificat (Luke 1:49). After the birth of John the Baptist, his father, Zechariah, is filled with the Spirit and foretells the fulfillment of God's promises and the dawning of salvation through the forgiveness of sins (Luke 1:67–79). The association of Mary, the Spirit, and the gift of prophecy continues in Luke's account of Mary's presentation of the child Jesus in the temple. The Spirit is upon Simeon, and he blesses God and speaks a word of prophecy to Mary. His prophetic recognition of Jesus as the Messiah is confirmed by the prophetess Anna (Luke 2:25–38).

This initial outpouring of the Spirit upon Mary bequeathed lasting gifts to the Church in the Spirit-filled prophetic prayers spoken by Mary and those around her. We repeat Elizabeth's inspired prophetic words in the rosary when we bless Mary. In the Liturgy of the Hours, these inspired words become part of our daily prayer. We recite Zechariah's *Benedictus* in morning prayer, join Mary in her Magnificat in evening prayer, and conclude the day with the *Nunc Dimittis*, the inspired prayer of the prophet Simeon.

These initial signs of the Spirit's presence do not appear again through the rest of Luke's Gospel. Luke emphasizes the Spirit's anointing upon Jesus, but he does not speak again of others who are filled with the Spirit and who prophesy until he begins the Book of Acts. While these visible signs of the gift of the Spirit abate for a while, Mary continues to treasure all these things in her heart, contemplating these mysteries (Luke 2:51). Having received the Spirit and witnessed his gifts poured out upon those around her, she will eventually help the Church receive the Spirit and his gifts by her intercession in the upper room at Pentecost (Acts 1:14). John Paul II sees Mary's presence in the upper room as revealing her special role as the spouse of the Spirit who has received the fullness of the Spirit's presence and now prays for the outpouring of his gifts upon the Church (6/28/1989). Mary is our model for receptivity to the Spirit and his gifts. She assists us by her intercession to open our hearts and minds to the Spirit.

## John the Baptist Announces the Baptism of the Spirit

Both Mary and John the Baptist provide a bridge from the Old Covenant to the New. Mary is the faithful daughter of Zion who fulfills the mission of Israel in her "yes" to the promises of God. She is, at the same time, the first and preeminent member of the Church, the first to welcome and receive Christ. John the Baptist is the last of the prophets of Israel. "In him, the Holy Spirit concludes his speaking through the prophets" (*CCC* 719). At the same time, John announces the new outpouring of the Spirit, proclaiming Christ as the one who "baptizes with the Holy Spirit" (Matthew 3:11, Mark 1:8, Luke 3:16, and John 1:33)

This phrase "baptism in the Spirit" announced by John the Baptist and repeated by the risen Lord (Acts 1:5) expresses the gift of the Spirit in all its dimensions. The phrase should not be interpreted too narrowly but should be understood in its fullest application. "Baptism in the Holy Spirit" can be used to describe the universal mission of Jesus Christ as the one who pours out the fullness of the Spirit upon humanity. "Baptism in the Holy Spirit" can also refer more specifically to Pentecost, when the Spirit was given to the

Church. "Baptism in the Spirit" is also an appropriate description of our sacramental reception of the Spirit in baptism and confirmation. Finally, "baptism in the Spirit" can describe an experience in which we welcome the Spirit's presence, power, and gifts in our life.

John Paul II begins to unfold these various dimensions in a general audience on the baptism in the Holy Spirit (9/6/1989). First of all, John Paul II associates the baptism in the Spirit with the universal mission of Jesus. John the Baptist's announcement that Jesus will baptize in the Spirit can be understood in its widest sense as a description of the entire mission of Jesus as an outpouring of the Spirit upon humanity. John Paul further links the baptism in the Holy Spirit to Jesus' reference to his own death as his baptism. Jesus said he came to cast fire upon the earth and linked that coming fire to the baptism he must undergo. "I came to bring fire to the earth, and how I wish it were already kindled! I have a baptism with which to be baptized, and what stress I am under until it is completed" (Luke 12:49–50)! Jesus spoke here of the baptism of his suffering and death through which the baptism of the Spirit and fire would be poured out upon humanity. After Jesus endures the fire of the cross, the Spirit flows out to the world, "spreading the baptism of fire" that Jesus said he would cast upon the earth. Thus, "baptism in the Spirit" can have a universal significance as a way of expressing the renewal of humanity through the gift of the Holy Spirit poured out from the death and resurrection of Christ. This universal mission of Christ and the Spirit is realized in the Church. Thus, John Paul II's discussion moves from baptism in the Spirit as a description of Christ's mission to humanity to a more specific application of the phrase to the birth of the Church. John Paul II describes Pentecost as the Church's baptism in the Spirit. The fire that Jesus said he would kindle on the earth, the fire of the Holy Spirit, gives birth to the Church. The Church was baptized in the Spirit on the day of Pentecost, and that gift of the Spirit will remain with the Church to the very end of history. John Paul II moves from the universal baptism in the Spirit as the saving mission of Christ, through the ecclesial baptism of the Spirit as the birth of the Church at Pentecost, to our individual baptism in the Spirit through the sacraments. He concludes this audience on baptism in the Spirit by reference to the sacrament of baptism. In this first sacrament we are baptized in water and Spirit. By this sacrament, each of us shares individually in the universal and ecclesial meaning of baptism in the Spirit. We share in Christ's own baptism, dying and rising with him to new life in the Spirit. We receive the gift of the Spirit given to the Church at Pentecost. The Spirit who dwells in the Church comes to dwell in our hearts.

The sacrament of confirmation is also related to the baptism of the Spirit. Confirmation "perpetuates the grace of Pentecost in the Church" (CCC 1288). Baptism and confirmation are closely linked. Baptism is the "gateway to life in the Spirit" (CCC 1213). Confirmation completes baptism by the gift of the Spirit given through the laying on of hands and anointing with oil (CCC 1288–89). In the sacrament of baptism, the Spirit enables us to share in Christ's death and resurrection. In confirmation, Christ enables us to share fully in the gift of the Spirit. Confirmation brings baptismal grace to fulfillment by uniting us more firmly to Christ and his Church, increasing the gifts of the Spirit in us, sealing and marking us as Christ's own and strengthening us to be his witnesses. As that sacrament that perpetuates Pentecost, gives the fullness of the Spirit, grants an increase of spiritual gifts and empowerment for witness, we may speak of confirmation as a sacramental baptism in the Spirit.

Many also speak of the baptism of the Spirit as an experiential and charismatic outpouring of the Spirit received through prayer. Without denying that the whole Church was baptized in the Spirit at Pentecost or that we were baptized in the Spirit in the sacraments of baptism and confirmation, we may also recognize subsequent experiences of the Spirit's power and gifts as fresh baptisms of the Spirit. John Paul II speaks of an "always new" coming of the Holy Spirit brought about continually in individuals and in the Church through varied outpourings of the Spirit, including both sacramental and charismatic movements of the Spirit (11/21/1990). All of these are outpourings of the Spirit in which we receive him as gift. John Paul II speaks of Pentecost as initiating a process. The outpouring of the Spirit on Pentecost in the Book of Acts is quickly followed by a "new Pentecost event" in which the Spirit is once again manifested to the gathered disciples in a tangible way (11/29/1989). After facing persecution, the apostles and other disciples gather to pray, and once again they are filled with the Spirit (Acts 4:31–32). The experience of that first baptism of the Spirit on the day of Pentecost is repeated by new "Pentecosts" or fresh baptisms in the Spirit in the life of the Church. Likewise, in the life of individuals, our sacramental baptism in the Spirit can be renewed and experienced in a fresh outpouring of the Spirit as we surrender to him. Saint Paul wrote to Christians who had been baptized and sealed by the Spirit and encouraged them to "be filled with the Spirit" (Ephesians 5:18). He encouraged Saint Timothy to once again "stir into flame" that gift of the Spirit that he had received through the laying on of hands (2 Timothy 1:6). John Paul II emphasizes that the gift of the Holy Spirit is given to each of us as individual persons to be welcomed through "knowledge, conscious love and enjoyment of God as an inner guest" (3/20/1991). Some prefer to reserve the term "baptism in the Spirit" for the sacraments and like to call this experience a "renewal in the Spirit" or a "release of the Spirit." In this case, vocabulary is less important than the experience. Have we "quenched" the Spirit given to us in the sacraments? Then let us "stir into flame" the gift we have been given through persistent prayer for a fresh outpouring in our lives.

## Jesus Anointed by the Spirit

John the Baptist recognized Jesus as the one who would baptize in the Holy Spirit because he saw the Spirit come upon Jesus when he baptized him in water. All four Gospels witness to the descent of the Spirit upon Jesus in the form of a dove (Matthew 3:16, Mark 1:10, Luke 3:22, and John 1:32). Each Gospel adds certain illuminating details. The heavens are opened and the Spirit descends. Saint Mark speaks of this opening of heaven as a tearing or rending open, using the same words with which he later describes the tearing of the temple veil during Jesus' crucifixion (Mark 1:10 and 15:38). The barrier between heaven and earth erected by the sin of humanity is torn just like the temple veil as the Spirit descends upon Jesus at his baptism. The Spirit is given fully to Jesus. Saint John mentions that the Spirit not only descends upon Jesus, the Spirit "remains" with him and this Spirit is given to and given by Jesus in abundance, without measuring or rationing (John 3:34). Saint Luke mentions that, after his baptism, as Jesus was praying, the Holy Spirit descended upon him (Luke 3:21–22). Jesus models that prayer for the Holy Spirit, which he encourages us to pray elsewhere in Luke's Gospel (Luke 11:9–13).

Jesus was conceived by the Spirit in the womb of the Blessed Virgin Mary (Luke 1:35). By the Spirit, his human nature was fully united to his divine person and filled with every grace of the Spirit from his conception. So, he is not receiving the Spirit for the first time in his baptism. At his baptism, Jesus receives the visible anointing of the Spirit for his mission as prophet, priest, and king. Like prophets, priests, and kings of the Old Testament, Jesus is anointed for his threefold office. Those figures in the Old Testament who prefigure Jesus' three offices were anointed by men, but Jesus is anointed by God. "God anointed Jesus of Nazareth with the Holy Spirit and with power" (Acts 10:38). Jesus fulfills the prophetic psalm that declared, "God, your God, has anointed you with the oil of gladness beyond your companions" (Psalm 45:7, cited in Hebrews 1:9). John baptizes him with water, but the Spirit himself descends upon Jesus to anoint him. This is where Jesus derives the title, "Christ." "Christ" is the Greek term for "messiah," which means anointed one. Jesus receives this anointing, not only to fulfill his own messianic mission but also in order to share that anointing with his followers. To be Christian is to be anointed by the Holy Spirit, to be a "little Christ." Everyone baptized Christian is given a share in the prophetic, priestly, and kingly mission of Jesus and receives the anointing of the Spirit to fulfill that mission (*CCC* 695, 783). The abundant anointing of the Spirit resting and remaining on Christ flows from Christ the head to all members of his body. Novation, in the third-century work, *On the Trinity*, says the Holy Spirit "came and abode upon" Jesus, dwelling in him "full and entire," unlimited by "any measure or portion" that the Spirit might "overflow copiously" so that others might "receive some enjoyment of his graces" as "streams of gifts and works" of the Spirit continuously flowing from Christ to all his members.

Jesus begins his public ministry with the proclamation that he has been anointed by the Holy Spirit in fulfillment of Isaiah's prophesy of the coming Spirit-anointed Messiah (Luke 4:16–21). He casts out demon spirits in the power of the Holy Spirit as a sign that he is inaugurating the promised kingdom of God (Matthew 12:28). In his preaching, Saint Peter sums up the entire public ministry of Jesus in light of his anointing by the Holy Spirit:

> You know the message…how God anointed Jesus of Nazareth with the Holy Spirit and with power; how he went about doing good and healing all who were oppressed by the devil, for God was with him (Acts 10:36–38).

## Jesus' Teachings on the Holy Spirit in the Synoptic Gospels

Jesus teaches on the Holy Spirit in the context of the opposition to his ministry that he faced and that his disciples would face. Responding to those who oppose his ministry, Jesus warns against blaspheming the Holy Spirit. Preparing his disciples for the opposition and persecution they will face, Jesus promises the assistance of the Holy Spirit.

When Jesus begins healing the sick and casting out demons, those who oppose him accuse him of casting out demons by the power of demons. Jesus cautions his critics not to attribute to the devil the works of the Spirit that he is performing. It is in this context that he warns them not to sin against the Holy Spirit, saying, "people will be forgiven for every sin and blasphemy, but blasphemy against the Spirit will not be forgiven" (Matthew 12:31, Mark 3:29, and Luke 12:10). In the immediate context, this blasphemy against the Spirit refers to those who reject the presence of the Holy Spirit at work in Jesus and attribute the Spirit's presence to the work of the devil. Christ is offering deliverance from evil through the gift of the Holy Spirit, and they reject his gift. We can see from this that blasphemy against the Spirit is not a matter of mere words or even of a singular act, but rather describes a persistent and stubborn rejection of the healing presence of the Spirit working through Jesus. At its heart, the blasphemy against the Spirit is the rejection of the gift of the Spirit, whom Christ sends to free us from the devil's power. John Paul II explains that blasphemy against the Holy Spirit consists in "the refusal to accept the salvation which God offers to man through the Holy Spirit...the radical refusal to accept this forgiveness, of which he is the intimate giver" (DEV 46). There is no sin, no matter how serious, that cannot be forgiven. The unforgivable sin to which Jesus refers is the refusal to be forgiven! There are no limits to the mercy of God, but God's mercy must be received. Through the gift of the Holy Spirit, God offers us forgiveness of sins and the grace of conversion. If one refuses this offer of mercy by stubborn resistance to the Spirit and persists in that refusal to death, then and only then is one in danger of this unforgivable blasphemy against the Holy Spirit (CCC 982, 1037, 1864).

As Jesus sends his disciples out to proclaim forgiveness of sins, he warns them that they will receive the same opposition as their master. He warns them that they will be taken before synagogues, councils, kings, and rulers. However, Jesus encourages them to have no anxiety when they are called upon to speak before their persecutors, for the Holy Spirit will give them the words to say (Matthew 10:19–20, Mark 13:11, and Luke 12:11–12 and 21:14–15). In many parts of the world today, Christians still face such persecution and learn to rely on the help of the Holy Spirit to testify for Christ in the face of martyrdom. For most of this book's readers, however, we will not be called upon to die for Christ. Still, we often face the world's opposition in the form of rejection, ridicule, and exclusion. The promise of Jesus is there for us as well. The Holy Spirit will give us the words to say and empower us with the courage to witness for Christ even in the face of opposition.

## Jesus' Teaching on the Spirit in the Gospel of John

The fullest teaching of Jesus on the Holy Spirit is found in the Gospel of John. Jesus begins to reveal the coming gift of the Holy Spirit in his one-on-one conversations with those he encounters. To Nicodemus, he speaks of a new birth through water and Spirit (John 3:5). To the Samaritan woman at the well, Jesus offers the "living water" of the Spirit (John 4:13–14). Jesus publicly declares the coming outpouring of the Spirit in the temple during the celebration of the Jewish feast of Tabernacles. On the last day of that feast, the Jewish high priest would take water and pour it over the altar. On that very day, Jesus called all who thirst to come to him and receive rivers of living water (John 7:37–39). Depending on how the passage is translated and punctuated, Jesus is either speaking of rivers of living water that will flow out of those who believe in him or he is speaking of the rivers of living water that will flow out of his own heart. The *New Jerusalem Bible* preserves this ambiguity in its translation: Let anyone who believes in me come and drink! As Scripture says, "From his heart shall flow streams of living water" (John 7:38, *New Jerusalem Bible*).

The phrase "as Scripture says" does not refer to a specific Old Testament passage but to various passages read during the feast of Tabernacles that speak of God's gift of the Spirit as life-giving water (Zechariah 14:8, and Ezekiel 47:1). If the "heart" refers to the heart of Jesus, we can see this passage fulfilled later in John, when the heart of Jesus is pierced and out of his heart flows blood and water (John 19:34). This water and blood symbolizes the Spirit, baptism, and Eucharist that flow from the pierced heart of Jesus giving birth to the Church as his bride (*CCC* 694, 1225). This explains why, after recalling Jesus' words at the feast of Tabernacles, John adds the comment,

"Now he said this about the Spirit, which believers in him were to receive; for as yet there was no Spirit, because Jesus was not yet glorified" (John 7:39). The Spirit, the promised advocate from heaven, is to be given through Jesus' glorification upon the cross. This is why Jesus tells the disciples, "it is to your advantage that I go away, for if I do not go away, the Advocate will not come to you; but if I go, I will send him to you" (John 16:7). Jesus' going away, his death, brings about our salvation and then all that he accomplishes in his death and resurrection is brought to us by the Holy Spirit. When Jesus says the Spirit "will take what is mine and declare it to you" (John 16:14), we should understand this to refer to the Spirit taking all that Christ is and all that he accomplishes for us in his death and resurrection and bringing that to us. The Spirit enables us to share in the paschal mystery of Christ and the salvation it provides.

In the upper room, just prior to his death, Jesus speaks more fully to his disciples about this coming gift of the Holy Spirit. He tells them that the Spirit who has been with them will come to dwell within them (John 14:17). Jesus describes the Spirit as the Paraclete (advocate, helper, defender, comforter, counselor) who will not leave the disciples as orphans but will come to comfort and strengthen them. The Paraclete is the Spirit of truth who will guide the apostles into all truth, bringing to their remembrance all that Jesus taught in the past and showing them things to come in the future (John 14:26 and 16:12–13).

The Spirit of truth will also "convince the world of sin." It is very important that we have a proper understanding of this ministry of the Spirit. He convinces us of sin in order to deliver us from sin and heal us from the effects of sin. Saint John says the Holy Spirit will convince the world of "sin and righteousness and judgment" (John

16:8). John Paul II explains these terms as follows: Sin refers to the sin of the world in rejecting God's gifts, the initial gift of creation and the further gift of his Son. Only the Spirit who is gift and truth can show us how we sin by rejecting God's gift and disobeying his truth. Righteousness refers to the definitive righteousness of Jesus Christ offered to us as gift. Judgment refers to the definitive judgment upon sin and Satan accomplished by the death and resurrection of Jesus Christ. The Spirit, who is gift, shows us the foolishness of our sin in rejecting God's gifts and leads us to the gift of forgiveness offered to us in the paschal mystery (DEV 27–45). We should not resist the Spirit when he shows us our sins, for he does so out of love, that we might bring those sins into his light and in that light find forgiveness and healing. John Paul II emphasizes that the Spirit of truth convinces the world of sin for the good of humanity in order to lead us to salvation through Christ (5/24/1989).

## The Holy Spirit and the Cross

Jesus offers himself upon the cross through the Holy Spirit. Jesus Christ, "through the eternal Spirit," offered himself to God (Hebrews 9:14). There were Old Testament sacrifices in which fire from heaven consumed the sacrifice (Leviticus 9:24, 1 Kings 18:38, and 2 Chronicles 7:1). John Paul II describes the Holy Spirit as the "fire from heaven" that comes upon the sacrifice of Christ and takes that sacrifice into the communion of the Trinity:

> The Holy Spirit as love and gift comes down, in a certain sense, into the very heart of the sacrifice that is offered on the cross.…He consumes this sacrifice with the fire of the love that unites the Son with the Father in the Trinitarian communion (DEV 41).

The cross and Pentecost are united by the Spirit. John Paul II calls us to discover the fire of the Spirit within the cross and flowing from the cross as the power of service poured out upon the Church at Pentecost, leading us into communion with the triune God (8/1/1990).

The Holy Spirit comes down upon the sacrifice of Christ and then flows from that sacrifice to us. The Gospel of John explains that the Spirit is given when Jesus is glorified (John 7:39). John's Gospel also associates Jesus' glorification with the cross. Upon the cross, Jesus is lifted up, drawing all men to himself (John 3:14 and 12:32). The cross is the long-awaited "hour" of Jesus in which he glorifies the Father and the Father glorifies him (John 12:27). John recounts Jesus' death in these profound words: "Jesus…said, 'It is finished.' Then he bowed his head and gave up his spirit" (John 19:30). The phrase "his spirit" is, literally translated, "the spirit." John is not simply stating that Jesus breathed his last breath. In his dying, Jesus handed over to his Church the Spirit whom he had promised. From the cross of Jesus comes the Holy Spirit through whom we become sharers in that cross that leads to life. Having been glorified upon the cross, the risen Lord Jesus breathes out the Spirit again, giving the apostles the power to forgive sins (John 20:21–23). At the same time, as revealed by the Gospel of Luke, Jesus instructs the apostles to wait and to pray for a further and fuller outpouring of the Spirit that will fill them and the whole Church with power to proclaim the Gospel (Luke 24:49 and Acts 1:5, 8).

## Pentecost

On the day of Pentecost, the Spirit was poured out upon the apostles who had been praying with Mary in the upper room. The Spirit came upon them with the sound of a mighty wind. Tongues of fire appeared and rested on each one. They begin to pray in tongues, praising God in other languages. Peter, who before had fearfully denied and abandoned his Lord, now stood and courageously proclaimed Christ, saying: "Being therefore exalted at the right hand of God, and having received from the Father the promise of the Holy Spirit, [Jesus] has poured out this that you both see and hear" (Acts 2:33). The feast of Pentecost was a Jewish festival, originally celebrating the harvest but eventually understood also as a celebration of the giving of the covenant. Jews would recall on this day how God gave the Law to Moses on Mount Sinai. With the visible outpouring of the Spirit and the public manifestation of the birth of the Church, Pentecost becomes for Christians the celebration of the new covenant. When God came down upon Mount Sinai to offer the first covenant to Israel, there was a visible manifestation of fire (Exodus 19:18). So now once again, with the dawning of the new covenant, God is manifested by fire.

While the first covenant was only with Israel, this new covenant, the Spirit, is given to all the nations. This universality is manifested by the gift of many tongues, understood by visiting pilgrims from many nations. Saint Luke emphasizes this universality by his long list of nations represented by those who heard God praised in their native tongues: Parthians, Medes, Elamites, residents of Mesopotamia, Judea, Cappadocia, Pontus, Asia, Phrygia, Pamphylia, Egypt, Libya, Cyrene, Rome, Cretans, and Arabs (Acts 2:8–11). All of these nations heard the good news of Jesus Christ in their own language. In this gift of many tongues, leading to common understanding, Pentecost represents the reversal of Babel. In the Old Testament, God's judgment upon the tower of Babel led to the scattering of nations through the multiplication and confusion of languages (Genesis 11:5–9). At Pentecost, those from many nations are united in hearing God praised by the apostles. The unity, universality, and catholicity of the Church already manifested at Pentecost grows as the Spirit is successively poured out upon Jews, then Samaritans, then gentiles (Acts 2:41, 8:14–17, and 10:44–48).

The Church's baptism in the Spirit on Pentecost is an abiding reality. John Paul II says there is a sense in which the Church has never left the upper room. The Church never ceases to pray for the outpouring of the Holy Spirit, and she carries that prayer in her heart even as she goes forth on mission into the world (DEV 66). The Church never ceases to pray Come Holy Spirit, and the outpouring of the Spirit upon the praying Church continues unceasingly.

At Pentecost, the promises of the new covenant are fulfilled. John Paul II describes Pentecost as the "new beginning of God's self-giving in the Holy Spirit" (7/26/1989). In this gift of the Holy Spirit, all that Christ had accomplished in his death and resurrection is given to us. According to John Paul II, the divine self-giving in the new covenant has three dimensions: universality, interiority, and eternity. The Holy Spirit is universally poured out on all peoples; the Holy Spirit interiorly fills and transforms the human heart; and the gift of the Holy Spirit confirms the new covenant as the definitive and eternal covenant between God and humanity (8/2/1989).

Saint Luke describes the continuing movement of the Spirit through the history of the early Church in Acts. Some would say that this book, rather than bearing the title, Acts of the Apostles, should be renamed the Acts of the Holy Spirit. Through this book, Saint Luke describes the Spirit as repeatedly "given," "falling upon," and "poured out" upon the Church. Those who respond to this gift, "receive" the Spirit, are "filled" with the Spirit, become "full" of the Spirit. By the Spirit, the Church proclaims the Gospel, ordains leaders, and performs miracles. The Church and its members are guided by the Spirit.

## The Holy Spirit in the Letters of Saint Paul

Saint Luke's history of the Spirit-filled Church is confirmed by the letters of Saint Paul. The centrality of the Spirit in the Church is reflected by the pervasive Spirit language in Saint Paul's letters. Saint Paul uses the word Spirit (*pneuma*) 145 times in his letters. While some of those refer to angelic or human spirits, the vast majority of the citations refer to the divine Spirit. Saint Paul uses a variety of names for the Holy Spirit. He refers to him as the Spirit, the Holy Spirit, the Spirit of God, the Spirit of the Lord, as well as the Spirit of Christ, the Spirit of Jesus Christ or the Spirit of the Son. The Spirit, as Spirit of God (the Father) and Spirit of Christ (the Son) brings us into communion with the Holy Trinity. Twice Saint Paul refers to the Spirit as uniting us to the Son in his intimate prayer to the Father as *abba* (Romans 8:15 and Galatians 4:6). Saint Paul describes the Holy Spirit as the Spirit of holiness, of life, of adoptive sonship, of unity, of promise, of wisdom and revelation, of redemption, of power, love, and discipline. He attributes all of the Church's gifts, charisms, and ministries to the Holy Spirit. Most of the time, when Saint Paul uses the adjective "spiritual," it should be capitalized as "Spiritual," despite the common tendency of most Bible translations to use lowercase. For example, when Saint Paul prays that we might be filled with "spiritual wisdom," he prays for us to receive wisdom that comes from the Spirit. When he speaks of "spiritual gifts," he refers to gifts given by the Spirit, and when he refers to a "spiritual person," he describes someone filled with the Spirit.

Saint Paul repeatedly associates the gift of the Spirit with baptism, Christian initiation, and salvation. Christians are washed, sanctified, and justified in the name of Jesus and by the Holy Spirit. In the washing of baptism we are made holy by the power of Jesus' name and the gift of the Holy Spirit (1 Corinthians 6:9–11). We are saved by the washing of baptism and renewal in the Spirit poured out upon us by Jesus Christ (Titus 3:4–5). Saint Paul reminds the Galatians of their conversion when they received the Spirit by faith, and he was sent into their hearts to make them children of God (Galatians 1:2 and 4:6). Saint Paul gives thanks to God for those in Thessalonica who were saved through belief in the truth of Jesus Christ and sanctification by the Spirit (2 Thessalonians 2:13). The Spirit makes us one through our common baptism. We are all baptized by the Spirit into the body of Christ (1 Corinthians 12:13). For Saint Paul, salvation, baptism, and Christian conversion is a Trinitarian event. The Father sends his Son to redeem us and adopt us as his children and then sends the Spirit into our hearts to make us sons and daughters (Galatians 4:4–6). Long before the Church develops a dogmatic formulation of the doctrine of the Trinity, Saint Paul describes the experience of salvation in the language of Trinitarian experience.

Saint Paul understands the Holy Spirit as the indwelling presence of God. It is the divine indwelling of the Spirit that makes us the temple of God. Saint Paul applies this temple language to both the Church as a whole and to individual members of the Church. Speaking of the entire Church, the body of Christ, as a temple, Saint Paul urges his readers not to destroy this temple through division and disunity (1 Corinthians 3:16–17). Elsewhere, Saint Paul speaks of us individually, in our physical bodies, as members of Christ's body and individual temples of the Spirit. In this context, he warns his readers not to violate the temple of their body through sexual immorality (1 Corinthians 6:15–20). In both cases, he emphasizes that the temple belongs to God and is made holy by his indwelling presence. Saint Paul exhorts us not to "grieve" this most holy guest who makes us into a living temple for God (Ephesians 4:30).

The indwelling Spirit is a sign of the dawning of the last days, the coming of the Messiah, and the resurrection from the dead. Saint Paul recognizes that these promises, as fulfilled by Christ, are characterized by a "now but not yet." Christ now reigns as Messiah and has sent forth the promised Holy Spirit, but we await the full consummation of his reign at his Second Coming. The resurrection has begun with the resurrection of Christ, but we still await the general resurrection of the dead at Christ's return. Saint Paul associates the Spirit with the "now" of fulfillment pointing toward the "not yet" of still fuller realization. The Spirit is the first fruits of salvation (Romans 8:23). We await the final harvest and the full fruit of salvation that we will realize in the resurrection of the body and eternal life in heaven. However, we already experience the fruits of redemption in this life through the gift of the Holy Spirit. The Spirit is the power of the resurrection already at work within us, raising us from the spiritual death of bondage to sin into the freedom of new life in Christ. The presence of the Spirit gives assurance of our future resurrection. "If the Spirit of him who raised Jesus from the dead dwells in you, he who raised Christ Jesus from the dead will give life to your mortal bodies also through his spirit who dwells in you" (Romans 8:11). The Spirit is God's seal, marking us as belonging to him and assuring us that he will fulfill his promises to us. We are "marked with the seal of the promised Holy Spirit….This is the pledge of our inheritance" (Ephesians 1:13–14). Our inheritance as children of God is the resurrection of the body and life with God in heaven. The seal of the Holy Spirit is the "pledge" of that promise. The Greek word *arrabon*, translated "pledge" or in some translations "guarantee," is taken from the ancient business world where it refers to a "down payment." The present gift of the Spirit is a promissory payment from God, assuring us that there is more to come, the future resurrection of our bodies and life with him in heaven (2 Corinthians 1:22, 5:5, and Ephesians 1:14). The Spirit is the Father's initial installment payment toward our full redemption, body and soul. The Holy Spirit is not only God's initial gift "to" us; it is also his down payment "for" us. Having made a down payment, God now claims us as his own. Once I make a down payment on a car, that car belongs to me. That down payment is my promise to return with the rest of the money, and the car lot cannot sell it to anyone else. Even so, we belong to God. The Father has purchased us first of all by the ransom paid by the blood his Son shed for us in his death for our sins. God then takes possession of us by the down payment of his indwelling Spirit within us. "Do you not know that your body is a temple of the Holy Spirit within you, which you have from God? You are not your own; you were bought with a price. So glorify God in your body" (1 Corinthians 6:19–20). We live in the hope of the future glorification of our bodies in the resurrection and live our present life in the body for God's glory. God assures us that he will fulfill his promises by "putting his seal on us and giving us his Spirit in our hearts as a first installment" (2 Corinthians 1:22).

The Spirit dwelling within us grants us the power to live a holy life. Saint Paul describes the "Spirit of Life" as a power within us that enables us to overcome the pull of temptation and sin. He describes the conflict between the Spirit and sin as two opposing laws. "The Law of the Spirit of Life in Christ Jesus has set me free from the law of sin and death" (Romans 8:2). Sin is described here as a law or principle at work to draw us down to death. The Spirit introduces a higher law or principle that counteracts sin and raises us up to new life in Christ.

The Holy Spirit reshapes our lives into the image of Jesus Christ. After referring to the law of the Spirit of Life, Saint Paul describes how the Spirit shapes our lives into the image of Christ the Son of the Father. We who are led by the Spirit are "children of God" because we have received the Spirit of adoption through whom we cry out, "Abba, Father!" (Romans 8:14–16). As children of God, we are heirs of Christ, sharing in the glory he inherits (Romans 8:17). However, in order to inherit that glory, we must allow the Spirit to shape our lives in the form of Christ's life of self-emptying love. The Spirit shapes our lives in cruciform imitation of Christ. We must suffer with Christ in order to be glorified with him (Romans 8:17). We share in his cross when we "put to death the deeds of the body" by the Spirit (Romans 8:13). Through our receptivity to the work of the Spirit in our lives, our lives will be reshaped into the image of Christ, the Son of the Father, who poured out his life in love for God and others.

The law of the Spirit of life not only reshapes our lives in the image of Jesus Christ, the Spirit also gives us the power to live this life, overcoming the temptation of sin. The Holy Spirit is the power of the resurrection, which gives life and strength and energy to live a life of love (Romans 8:9–11). "The Spirit helps us in our weakness; for we do not know how to pray as we ought, but that very Spirit intercedes with sighs too deep for words" (Romans 8:26). In our weakness against that law of sin and death that pulls us down, we need only pray for the Spirit's help to allow the Spirit to pray for us, in us, and through us. Through that prayer, the Spirit will release his energy into our lives, reshaping us into the image of Christ and empowering us to follow Christ.

## The Holy Spirit in the Letters of Peter, John, and Jude

We will conclude our survey of biblical teaching on the Holy Spirit by leaving Paul and considering some of the other epistles of the New Testament. We find a few significant references to the Spirit in the Letters of Saint Peter, Saint John and in the often-neglected and overlooked Epistle of Saint Jude.

Saint Peter refers to the Spirit as the "Spirit of Christ" who was already at work in the prophets of the Old Testament, mysteriously foretelling the coming suffering and glorification of the Messiah (1 Peter 1:11). Already in his hidden working in the Old Testament, the Spirit does not teach about himself but speaks of Christ, the one who is to come. The Holy Spirit inspired both the Old Testament prophets who foretold the coming of Christ and the apostles who proclaimed Christ after his coming. Like Saint Paul, Saint Peter describes the experience of salvation in Trinitarian language. We are chosen by the Father, sanctified by the Spirit, and cleansed by the blood of Jesus that we might follow him in obedient discipleship (1 Peter 1:2). That discipleship will lead to suffering, but when we suffer, Saint Peter, says, the Spirit of God and glory will rest upon us (1 Peter 4:14).

Saint John, in his first epistle, speaks of the Holy Spirit as the anointing, the illuminative indwelling presence of the Spirit of truth (1 John 2:27). The Holy Spirit is the interior teacher who teaches each of us from within. This interior teaching is not contrary to the teachings of the Church, for those who are taught by the Spirit are recognized by their faithfulness and docility to the teachings of the apostles (1 John 4:6). There were false prophets around when John wrote this letter, and he warns his readers to "test the Spirits." The true Spirit guides us to the truth about Christ, who came in the flesh and leads us to love our brothers and sisters (1 John 4:2, 7). John Paul II explains how this interior anointing of the Holy Spirit within us illumines our understanding and guides us in applying the Gospel to our individual lives. Through the interior teaching of the Holy Spirit, the truth does not remain merely abstract and speculative, but the Holy Spirit applies the words of Jesus to the concrete circumstances of our lives and directs us along the path of the Father's plan for our lives (4/24/1991).

In the First Epistle of Saint John, the Spirit dwelling within us is our assurance that Christ abides within us and we abide in him (1 John 3:24 and 4:13). The Spirit dwelling within us is manifested by love. Through the Spirit we come to know the love that the Father has shown to us by sending his Son in the flesh. We receive that love in the Spirit and respond to that love by loving one another (1 John 4:6–7 and 11–13).

The epistles of John are followed by one of the last and shortest books of the New Testament, the Epistle of Saint Jude. Jude encourages us to build ourselves up in our holy faith, to keep ourselves in the love of God and the mercy of Jesus Christ by praying in the Holy Spirit (Jude 1:20–21). Saint Paul also encourages us to "pray in the Spirit" (Ephesians 6:18). We pray in the Spirit when we acknowledge our weakness and allow the Holy Spirit to assist us in our prayer. Praying in the Spirit is praying in the presence of God. We pray with awareness, given by the Spirit, of the God to whom we pray. The Spirit will take our weak words, sighs, and groans and unite them to Jesus' prayer to the Father. Praying in the Spirit may take many forms. "To be sure, there are as many paths of prayer as there are persons who pray, but it is the same Spirit acting in all and with all" (*CCC* 2672). The Spirit may give us charisms like praying in tongues or inspired words of wisdom and knowledge in which we pray back to God with the words he inspires within us. The Spirit may lead us to silently and lovingly gaze upon Jesus in contemplative prayer. We may pray the Liturgy of the Hours in the Spirit, speaking to God with the Holy Spirit's own inspired words in the psalms. In the Mass, we join in the Spirit-filled prayer of the Church where the Spirit unites us to one another and to Christ in thanksgiving to the Father.

## A Closing Invitation in the Book of Revelation

In one of the last verses of the last book of the Bible, the New Testament closes with an invitation to receive the Spirit. (The quoted passages in this paragraph are from Revelation 22:17.) Together with the Spirit, the Church prays for the coming of Christ. "The Spirit and the bride say, 'Come.'" Those who hear the Church's invitation are invited to join in that prayer as well. "And let everyone who hears say, 'Come.'" And then all who thirst for God are invited to come receive the free gift of his Spirit: "And let anyone who is thirsty come. Let anyone who wishes take the water of life as a gift." Thus, Scripture ends with an invitation to drink deeply of the Spirit who quenches our thirst for God.

## REFLECTION QUESTIONS

1. *How is the Spirit both revealed and hidden in the Old Testament?*

2. *How does the coming of the Spirit to Mary foreshadow his coming to the Church at Pentecost?*

3. *What does John the Baptist mean when he says Jesus will baptize in the Spirit? Have you ever experienced a fresh baptism in the Spirit in your life?*

4. *How is the Holy Spirit present in the ministry of Jesus? In his death on the cross? In his resurrection?*

5. *What are the connections between Pentecost and the giving of the Law at Mount Sinai? What is the difference between the Old Testament story of Babel and the New Testament account of Pentecost?*

6. *What do you find to be the most helpful insights into the person and work of the Holy Spirit in the New Testament letters of Saint Paul and others?*

CHAPTER 3

# The Presence of the Spirit in the Church

## *The Church as the Place Where We Know the Spirit*

The Church is the place where we know the Holy Spirit. In his work, *Against Heresies*, Saint Irenaeus says, "the gift of God has been entrusted to the Church, as breath was to the first created man....For where the Church is, there is the Spirit of God, and where the Spirit of God is, there is the Church." The Holy Spirit is "revealed and given" to the Church at Pentecost, and we come to know the Spirit as we "recognize and welcome" him within the life of the Church (*CCC* 686). The Spirit given to the Church at Pentecost remains with the Church as an illuminating, sanctifying, and animating presence. The Holy Spirit is the "soul" of the Church, invisibly present and active within the body of Christ, just as our soul is invisibly present and active in our bodies.

That is not to limit the wind of the Spirit or to deny his universal presence but simply to identify where we can come to know and welcome him in his fullness. On the one hand, there is no limit to the Spirit's presence and activity. John Paul II emphasized that there is not one moment of history nor even one remote corner of creation where the Spirit is not present and working. At the same time, he also emphasized that the Church has been given the special mission to transmit to humanity the fullness of the Spirit received at Pentecost (8/12/1998). The universal presence of the Spirit in human history is often indistinct. The Spirit is widely experienced as a spiritual presence, but not known as a person. Within this universal history of the presence of the Spirit in the world, the Church bears a special witness to the Spirit. The Church is the sacramental sign and instrument of the offer of salvation of humanity through the Incarnation of the Word and the outpouring of the Spirit. To share the riches of the Spirit with all humanity, those of us who belong to the Church must first come to recognize and welcome this Spirit as he is present and giving himself to us in the Church. The catechism lists the following ways in which we know the Holy Spirit in the Church:

- in the Scriptures he inspired;
- in the tradition, to which the Church Fathers are always timely witnesses;
- in the Church's magisterium, which he assists;
- in the sacramental liturgy, through its words and symbols,

- ✎ in prayer, wherein he intercedes for us;
- ✎ in the charisms and ministries by which the Church
  is built up;
- ✎ in the signs of apostolic and missionary life;
- ✎ in the witness of saints through whom he manifests
  his holiness and continues the work of salvation
  (*CCC* 688).

An examination of each of these points will lead us into a fuller knowledge of the Holy Spirit through his presence and activity in the Church. With each of these, we are called to recognize the presence of the Spirit in the Church, and we are invited to welcome the Spirit into our lives so that we might come to know him better. We recognize the wind of the Spirit by observing the effects of his moving through the Church, and we welcome him into our lives as we open our hearts to his gifts.

## The Holy Spirit and Scripture

The Holy Spirit has a threefold relationship to the Holy Scriptures: He is the divine origin of the Scriptures, he guides us in the interpretation of the Scriptures, and he makes possible our own receptivity and response to the Scriptures as the living voice of God.

Encouraging his spiritual son, Timothy, to read the Scriptures, Saint Paul speaks of their origin in divine inspiration: "All scripture is inspired by God and is useful for teaching, for reproof, for correction, and for training in righteousness" (2 Timothy 3:16). "Inspired" means "God breathed." "Sacred Scripture is the speech of God as it is put down in writing under the breath of the Holy Spirit" (*CCC* 81). The Spirit is the divine breath that moves and guides the human authors of the Bible. "No prophecy ever came by human will, but men and women moved by the Holy Spirit spoke from God" (2 Peter 1:21). By his inspiration, the Spirit works through the human authors to communicate God's words. The human authors are not reduced to mere automatons or secretaries taking dictation. Rather, the Spirit works mysteriously in and through their human personalities, using their human experience, expressing God's word through their particular literary styles, communicating divine truth within the historical and cultural contexts in which these human authors lived and wrote. This shows us something about how the Holy Spirit works. The Holy Spirit does not negate, ignore, or otherwise bypass our humanity, but our human nature, suffused and interpenetrated by the breath of the Spirit, becomes capable of bearing and communicating the divine. The Holy Spirit chose certain men and acted "in them and by them" to communicate what God "wanted written," but in such a way that they "made full use of their own faculties and powers" and wrote "as true authors" (*CCC* 106). Thus, there is a dual authorship to Scripture. God is the author of Scripture because these writings are inspired by the Holy Spirit, but because of the manner in which the Holy Spirit works through the individual humanity of each inspired author, they, too, are "true authors."

This is important for understanding how the Spirit speaks to us in the Scriptures. In Scripture, the Holy Spirit "speaks to man in a human way." To understand what the Spirit is saying, we must "be attentive to what the human authors truly wanted to affirm." To do this we must "take into account the conditions of their time and culture, the literary genres in use at the time, and the modes of feeling, speaking and narrating then current" (*CCC* 109–110). This is why we can benefit from Bible dictionaries, commentaries and other tools in which scholars illuminate the historical and cultural context of the human authors for our understanding of the text. We discern the message of the divine author through the human authors. We cannot bypass the "human way" in which the Holy Spirit speaks to us in Scripture. We welcome the Spirit as we come to recognize his voice as he speaks through the varied human voices of Scripture. The Spirit brings us into communion with John, Paul, Isaiah, Jeremiah, and the many other authors of the Scriptures to receive the message the Spirit imprinted upon their lives and their words.

Authentic Catholic biblical interpretation gives attention to both the human and divine authorship of the Scriptures. While attention to the human authors and their historical context is essential and often quite illuminating, the historical approach alone is incomplete. "Sacred Scripture must be read and interpreted in the light of the same Spirit by whom it was written" (*CCC* 111). We must attend to the human authors through whom the Spirit speaks. We must also attend to the Spirit, the divine author, by whom those human authors speak. The catechism provides three principles of scriptural interpretation that assist us to read Scripture in light of its divine authorship by the Spirit. Reading the Scriptures according to these three principles also provides us with three ways in which we receive and welcome the Spirit who inspires the Scriptures.

The first principle for reading Scripture in light of its divine author is to read within the context of the whole Bible. We must interpret each part of Scripture in light of the content and unity of the whole Bible. We must read Scripture not only historically but also canonically. We read Scripture within the context of the whole canon of Old Testament and New Testament books. While written by diverse human authors in diverse cultural and historical settings using diverse literary genres and styles, these diverse books are united by the one Spirit who inspired them all. The Spirit reveals the unity of the Bible in the plan of God that is fulfilled in Christ. The Spirit guides us to the knowledge of Christ as the heart of the Bible in which all the parts find their meaning (*CCC* 112, 128). We welcome the Spirit as we allow him to illumine our minds to grasp the unity of Scripture in the disclosure of God's love revealed in Christ.

The second principle of interpretation according to the Spirit is to read Scripture "within the living tradition of the whole Church" (*CCC* 113). The same Spirit who inspired the original authors of the biblical writings dwells within the Church and guides the Church in the interpretation of those writings. The Holy Spirit illumined the early Fathers of the Church to understand the Scriptures and has guided the magisterium to provide authentic guidance for our understanding of its message. Down through the ages the Spirit has inspired teachers whom the Church has acknowledged as "doctors of the Church" who can serve as reliable expositors of the biblical message. In the experience of the saints, the Holy Spirit has inspired living witnesses to truths of Scripture. In all of this rich tradition, the Holy Spirit provides a wealth of insight to illumine and guide our own reading of Scripture. We are encouraged by the Spirit not to read Scripture as isolated individuals but as part of the larger community of interpretation. We welcome the Spirit as he leads us into communion with the wisdom of those in the Church who have interpreted and meditated on the Scriptures down through the ages.

The third key to an authentic interpretation of Scripture based on its divine inspiration by the Spirit is the "analogy of faith" (*CCC* 114). This is a way of reading Scripture that looks for the connections between the various truths of the faith within the whole plan of divine revelation. Alert to the leading of the Spirit, we may experience the joy of theological discovery as we search for how one truth connects to and illuminates another. One passage of Scripture illumines another, and that passage sheds light on still others.

Each dogma of faith is connected to and illumines other dogmas. The truth of the Trinity illumines our understanding of Christ, the truth about Christ illumines our understanding of humanity, the truth about humanity illumines our understanding of the Blessed Virgin Mary, the truth about Mary illumines our understanding of the Church, and on and on. Divine truth is like a multifaceted crystal illumined by the Holy Spirit. We welcome the Spirit as we come to recognize the interconnections and interrelationships of one truth to another in the light of his illumination.

The Scriptures find their origin in the inspiration of the Spirit, and the Spirit guides us in the authentic interpretation of Scripture in light of its dual human and divine authorship. The Spirit also enables us to hear and respond to Scripture as the living, life-transforming message of God. The Spirit who first inspired the Scriptures accompanies the Scriptures as they are read. Saint Paul wrote about those whose minds are veiled to the meaning of Scripture and pointed to the Holy Spirit as the one who removes the veil and allows us "with unveiled faces" to behold "the glory of the Lord" and to be transformed into his likeness from day to day (2 Corinthians 3:12–18). The Spirit of God, who alone knows the deep things of God, grants us knowledge of the gifts that God has bestowed on us. These things cannot be discerned without the assistance of the Holy Spirit. Through the Holy Spirit we acquire the mind of Christ, a mind illumined and transformed by the knowledge of Christ as the fullness of divine revelation (2 Corinthians 2:10–16).

As we open our hearts to the Holy Spirit in our listening to Scripture at Mass, in praying the Scriptures in the liturgy, in our private reading and mediation on Scripture at home, the Spirit will make the biblical writings come alive and personal to us. Saint Augustine, prior to his conversion, heard a child's voice telling him to "take up and read." Opening the Scriptures at random, he read, "Put on the Lord Jesus Christ, and make no provision for the flesh, to gratify its desires" (Romans 13:14). The Holy Spirit took that one verse and penetrated Saint Augustine's heart with faith and the grace of conversion. He was soon baptized and went on to become a bishop and a saint. Saint Francis opened the Scriptures three times and read, "sell what you own...then come, follow me....Let them deny themselves and take up their cross and follow me....Take nothing for your journey" (Mark 10:21, Matthew 16:24, and Luke 9:3). In those passages he heard the call of the Holy Spirit to a new form of religious life characterized by radical poverty in following Christ. Perhaps not as dramatically, but just as personally, all Catholics can experience the Scriptures penetrating their heart as they read the Bible in the Spirit. The catechism encourages us to mobilize all of our faculties in meditation, engaging our "thought, imagination, emotion, and desires" in the spiritual reading or *lectio divina* of Scripture (*CCC* 2708). The Spirit helps us meditate on the Scriptures, contemplate the words in our hearts, and grasp their reality in spiritual experience.

It is also through the Holy Spirit that we find the power to say "yes" to God's word. In order to have the faith that assents to God's revelation we must have "the interior helps of the Holy Spirit, who moves the heart and converts it to God, who opens the eyes of the mind and 'makes it easy for all to accept and believe the truth'" (*CCC* 153). We come to know the Holy Spirit as our teacher as we allow him to illumine our minds with the truth of Scripture and open our hearts so he might transform us by those truths.

## The Holy Spirit in Tradition and the Magisterium

The Holy Spirit who inspired the Scriptures is given to the Church to guide her into all truth (John 16:13). Jesus promised the apostles that the Holy Spirit would teach them all things and bring to their remembrance all that he had said to them (John 14:26 and 16:13). Jesus did not commit his teachings to writing but entrusted his truth to the apostles and breathed the Holy Spirit upon them. Through that gift of the Spirit they would be able to transmit the truth of Christ in their teachings. Through the apostles and their successors, the bishops, the tradition of Jesus Christ is transmitted under the guiding light of the Holy Spirit. That is why the Church "does not derive her certainty about all revealed truths from Scripture alone" but from Scripture and Tradition together (*CCC* 81–82). Within the tradition, the popes and the bishops, as successors to Peter and the apostles, receive the help of the Holy Spirit to fulfill their ministry as shepherds and teachers of the faithful. By the power of the Holy Spirit they receive a special grace or charism of infallibility when they teach in a definitive manner on matters of faith and morality (*CCC* 890). It is through such gifts that the Holy Spirit works through the magisterium of the Church to guide the faithful into all truth.

When the early apostles gathered in Jerusalem to deliberate over crucial issues facing the Church of their day, they prefaced the concluding decisions of their council with the words, "It...seemed good to the Holy Spirit and to us" (Acts 15:28). They recognized the presence of the Spirit guiding their deliberations and giving divine approval to their decisions. That confidence in the guidance of the Holy Spirit has accompanied subsequent Church councils all the way from Nicea to Vatican II. In papal definitions, ecumenical councils and other expressions of the magisterium, the Holy Spirit assists these shepherds of the Church to fulfill their mission. When understood as the work of the Holy Spirit, the dogmas of faith proposed by the magisterium can be received as lights for the spiritual life, illuminating our path to God (*CCC* 88–89). The pope and the bishops have been made guardians of the Lord's flock by the Holy Spirit in order to feed the people of God (Acts 20:28). We welcome the Holy Spirit when we allow their teaching to feed us with God's truth and guide us in following his way.

By the Holy Spirit, the Church retains in her living tradition the memory of Jesus' life and teaching, not merely as written relics of the past but as the living presence of Christ in her midst. By the Spirit, the Church grows in her understanding of the truth of Christ, and doctrine develops. Taught by the Holy Spirit, the Church grows daily in deeper understanding. Tradition is the cumulative record of the teaching of the Spirit, guiding the Church in a growing comprehension of the revelation entrusted to her by Christ (*CCC* 66, 94).

> The Holy Spirit, who…keeps the memory of Christ alive in his Church…also leads her toward the fullness of truth and inspires new formulations expressing the unfathomable mystery of Christ at work in his Church's life (*CCC* 2625).

We find the voice of the Holy Spirit in the teachings of the Church down through the ages, from the Church Fathers to contemporary pronouncements of the magisterium.

The presence of the Spirit in the tradition goes beyond words, however. In its most comprehensive sense, tradition is that work of the Holy Spirit by which "the Church, in her doctrine, life, and worship perpetuates and transmits to every generation all that she herself is, all that she believes" (*CCC* 78). Tradition is not transmitted by doctrinal teachings alone, but by the entire life and worship of the Church. In this transmission of tradition, through the work of the Spirit, the Church not only hands on all that she believes, the Church transmits all that she is. By the presence of the Holy Spirit, our participation in the life and worship of the Church puts us into contact with tradition as a life-giving stream of truth and life. Within this stream, "the Father's self communication made through his Word in the Holy Spirit remains present and active in the Church" (*CCC* 79). We receive the Spirit as we recognize him as the source of that life and truth that flows through the traditions of the Church and welcome him as the one who transforms us by our participation in the teachings and practices of the Church that have been handed on to us.

## The Holy Spirit in the Liturgy and Sacraments

When Jesus met the Samaritan woman at the well, he spoke to her of the hour coming in which "true worshippers will worship the Father in spirit and truth" (John 4:23). We could probably capitalize the phrase "Spirit and Truth" as a reference to the Holy Spirit and Jesus Christ, the Incarnation of truth (John 14:6). Jesus points forward to the worship of the Church in which, united by the Spirit to his sacrifice, the Church will give praise to the Father in her sacraments and liturgy. It is the Holy Spirit who inspires our faith and worship, leading us to Christ, who, as our ever-living high priest, brings us to the Father. Liturgy is sometimes described as the "work of the people," but it is a work of a people inspired and animated by the Spirit. The liturgy is the "common work of the Holy Spirit and the Church" (*CCC* 1091). The catechism speaks of the work of the Spirit in the liturgical worship of the Church under three headings: the Spirit prepares our hearts to receive Christ, the Spirit recalls and makes present the mystery of Christ for us, and the Spirit brings us into communion with Christ and with one another.

The Spirit helps us prepare our hearts to be receptive to the grace offered in the Church's sacramental worship. "The grace of the Holy

Spirit seeks to awaken faith, conversion of heart, and adherence to the Father's will" (*CCC* 1098). When our hearts are awakened, moved to conversion, and drawn toward the Father in the liturgy, we are experiencing the wind of the Holy Spirit breathing his life into our souls.

The Spirit, as the "living memory of the Church," brings to our remembrance the events we celebrate in the liturgy and illumines our minds to understand their meaning. Through the Spirit, the Scriptures that are read and preached in the homily bring us into a living encounter with Christ. The Spirit illumines our minds to recognize how the events of the Old Covenant are fulfilled in the New Covenant (*CCC* 1094). The Spirit illumines our understanding and inspires our response of faith to God's word celebrated in the liturgy. The Holy Spirit illumines our minds to grasp the meaning and connections among the Scripture readings proclaimed in the liturgy and explained in the homily. As we welcome that illumination with thanksgiving, we recognize the presence of the Spirit.

The Spirit not only enables us to recall and understand the events we read in Scripture as events of the past, the Spirit brings the power of those events into the present. The history of salvation finds its center and climax in the death and resurrection of Jesus, the paschal mystery of his dying and rising for our salvation. Other events of the past happen and then pass away. "The paschal mystery of Christ, by contrast, cannot remain only in the past, because by his death he destroyed death, and all that Christ is—all that he did and suffered for all men—participates in the divine eternity, and so transcends all times while being made present in them all" (*CCC* 1085). The liturgy recalls the history of salvation culminating in the paschal mystery and, by the power of the Holy Spirit, actualizes that history in the present. In every celebration of the liturgy, "there is an outpouring of the Holy Spirit that makes the unique mystery present" (*CCC* 1104). We can recognize the wind of the Holy Spirit blowing through the liturgy and welcome him as we experience the death and resurrection of Christ as a present reality, carrying us from the death of our sinfulness to new life in the Spirit. When the distance between us and those past events seems to fade and we experience ourselves as participants in their saving power today, we are experiencing the Spirit's work in the liturgy.

Having prepared our hearts and recalled to our minds the events of salvation history, the Holy Spirit completes his work in the liturgy by bringing us into communion with God and with one another. First of all, the Spirit unites us to Christ. Christ is the divine vine and we are the branches. The Holy Spirit is the life-giving sap that flows from the vine to the branches and bears fruit within us (*CCC* 1108). The Spirit unites us to Christ and brings about our communion with him. In the liturgy, the Spirit moves the Church as bride of Christ to welcome her bridegroom. Each liturgy participates in and anticipates the final heavenly liturgy of the wedding feast of the lamb and his bride, the Church. In the liturgy, "the Spirit and the Bride say…Come Lord Jesus" (Revelation 22:17, 20). United to the Son, the Spirit leads us into communion with the Father. Through union with Christ in the Spirit, we have access to the Father, to whom our liturgical worship is directed (Ephesians 2:18). In this communion with the Father and the Son, the Holy Spirit unites us to one another. By one Spirit, we are baptized into one body made up of many members (1 Corinthians 12:12–13). By that same Spirit we are built together as one holy and living temple, a dwelling place of God made up of many living stones (1 Peter 2:4–5). In every celebration of the liturgy, the Spirit brings about this twofold communion with the Holy Trinity and with one another (*CCC* 1108).

In our understanding of the Mass, we focus, and rightly so, on the Real Presence of Christ. Yet, we should also remember the presence of the Holy Spirit in the Mass. There are two aspects of the Spirit's presence we would do well to keep in mind as we participate in the Mass. First of all, it is the Holy Spirit who transforms the bread and wine into the Body and Blood of Christ. Secondly, we not only receive Christ in holy Communion, we receive the Holy Spirit as well. The catechism cites Saint John of Damascus on the role of the Holy Spirit in the transformation of the bread and wine:

> You ask how the bread becomes the Body of Christ, and the wine...the Blood of Christ. I shall tell you: the Holy Spirit comes upon them and accomplishes what surpasses every word and thought (*CCC* 1106).

The Spirit brings about that transubstantiation of the bread and wine into the Body and Blood of Christ, through the words of the priest, spoken *in persona Christi*. Before, speaking the words of consecration, the priest holds his hands over the bread and wine in a gesture that signifies the overshadowing of the Spirit and prays for the Spirit to come upon these gifts. By the Spirit, the bread and wine are transformed into the substantial presence of Jesus Christ, Body and Blood, soul and divinity.

This prayer for the outpouring of the Holy Spirit upon our liturgical celebration is known as the Epiclesis (*CCC* 1105). The priest prays for the outpouring of the Holy Spirit upon our celebrations so that the Spirit might prepare our hearts to receive from God, recall to our minds the mysteries of salvation history in the past, make us partakers of those mysteries in the present, and bring us into communion with God and one another. This Epiclesis for the outpouring of the Holy Spirit is also a prayer that the liturgical celebration will bear fruit in our lives as we are sent forth from the liturgy to bear witness to Christ in the power of the Spirit:

> The Epiclesis is also a prayer for the full effect of the assembly's communion with the mystery of Christ....The Church therefore asks the Father to send the Holy Spirit to make the lives of the faithful a living sacrifice to God by their spiritual transformation into the image of Christ, by concern for the Church's unity, and by taking part in her mission through the witness and service of charity (*CCC* 1109).

The Spirit brings Christ to us in our celebration of the Eucharist. At the same time, when we receive Christ in the Eucharist, he brings the Spirit to us anew. Christ comes to us bringing a fresh anointing and outpouring of the Spirit into our souls. As we receive Christ in holy Communion, Christ comes to us as the bearer of the Spirit. Holy Communion not only renews our communion with Christ, but also our communion with the Holy Spirit. Saint Ephrem the Syrian writes in his hymns that "in the bread and cup are fire and Holy Spirit...whoever eats in faith, eats the Fire and Spirit." As we open our hearts to receive Christ in holy Communion, we should also open our hearts to the gift of the Holy Spirit given to us through our communion with Christ.

## The Holy Spirit and Prayer

The Holy Spirit's role in our prayer is not limited to liturgical worship. In our personal prayer, too, the Holy Spirit is the one from whom the prayer of the heart originates and the one who guides that prayer toward its goal—union with God. It is through the Spirit that we come to know the love of the Father revealed in Christ, and moved by the Spirit we cry out to the Father. "Because you are children, God has sent the Spirit of his Son into our hearts, crying, 'Abba, Father'" (Galatians 4:6)! By the Holy Spirit we come to know and experience the love of the Father, who has adopted us as his children in Jesus Christ. The Holy Spirit is the "Spirit of adoptive sonship" who inspires our prayer to the Father. The Spirit bears "witness with our spirit that we are children of God" (Romans 8:15–16).

Prayer does not begin with us but with God. The Holy Spirit is God's gift to awaken within us our response to his love. The Holy Spirit is the "living water welling up to eternal life in the heart that prays" (*CCC* 2652). The love of God poured into our hearts by the Holy Spirit (Romans 5:5) is the source of prayer. "Prayer...draws everything into the love by which we are loved in Christ and which enables us to respond to him by loving as he has loved us" (*CCC* 2658). John Paul II describes the Holy Spirit as the gift that enters our hearts when we pray. The Holy Spirit awakens prayer by making us aware of our deep need for God, the depth of the human heart that only God can fill. Then in response to our prayer, the Holy Spirit fills our hearts with his presence (DEV 65). Not only in formal liturgical prayer or in set times for prayer but in the events of each day, the Spirit makes prayer spring up from our hearts (*CCC* 2659). Thus, Saint Paul encourages us to "pray in the Spirit at all times" (Ephesians 6:18).

We pray to the Father, to the Son, and to the Spirit himself. The Holy Spirit inspires our prayer to the Father, he inspires our prayers to the Son, and by his inspiration, we cry out to the Spirit himself. First of all, the Spirit inspires our prayer to the Father. It is only by the gift of the Holy Spirit that we are able to call upon God as our Father. The catechism introduces the opening phrase of the "Our Father" by recalling the words of Saint Peter Chrysologus:

Our awareness of our status as slaves would makes us sink into the ground and our earthly condition would dissolve into dust, if the authority of our Father himself and the Spirit of his Son had not impelled us to this cry..."Abba, Father!"... When would a mortal dare call God 'Father,' if man's innermost being were not animated by power from on high (*CCC* 2777)?

The Spirit also draws us to the Son in prayer and gives us faith to call upon Jesus as our Lord. "Every time we begin to pray to Jesus it is the Holy Spirit who draws us on the way of prayer by his prevenient grace" (*CCC* 2670). It is by the power of the Holy Spirit that we are able to call upon Jesus as our Lord. The Spirit awakens the soul's love for the divine bridegroom and moves our hearts to seek him and cry out to him in prayer.

Since we are in such great need of the Spirit to help us pray, we also pray to the Spirit, asking him to come to us in our need. The Church teaches us to pray, "Come, Holy Spirit, fill the hearts of your faithful and enkindle in them the fire of your love" (*CCC* 2671). John Paul II recalls how his father taught him a prayer to the Holy Spirit when he was a young child and how he continued to faithfully pray that prayer daily through his life. The pope's personal secretary says that John Paul II, even though he could not speak, prayed this prayer with the help of others on his dying day. Perhaps this simple prayer was one of the secrets of the powerful life and ministry of this great pope. Recognizing our great need for the gifts and graces of the Spirit, we too should daily ask the Holy Spirit to come into our hearts afresh. Especially if we find prayer difficult, we should make our first prayer a simple cry to the Holy Spirit. The Spirit is given to help us in our weakness when we do not know how to pray, and the Spirit himself will pray for us, and in us, and through us (Romans 8:26).

The work of the Holy Spirit in prayer is universal. Following an interreligious gathering in Assisi in which followers of many religions came to pray for peace, John Paul II said, "Every authentic prayer is called forth by the Holy Spirit" (9/9/1998). In his encyclical on the Holy Spirit, John Paul II described the Holy Spirit as the "living breath of prayer" who is present "wherever people are praying in the world" (DEV 65). Wherever and whenever the desire for God is awakened, leading to prayer, that is a gift of the Holy Spirit. Saint Paul spoke of the whole of creation groaning for redemption in a prayer inspired by the Spirit's own desire (Romans 8:19–27). The Spirit is present in every sincere and virtuous prayer born out of genuine hunger for God, and through that prayer, the Spirit works to draw all to Christ, the Redeemer of the world. For those who, through no fault of their own, are ignorant of their need for Christ and his Church, the Holy Spirit, in a mysterious way known only to God, offers to all the possibility of partaking in the paschal mystery of Christ (*CCC* 1260).

We recognize and welcome the person of the Holy Spirit when we respond to the desire for God that he awakens in our hearts. When we find prayer difficult and ask the Spirit to help us in our weakness, when we allow the Spirit to purify our intentions in prayer, when we allow the Spirit to guide us in the journey of prayer toward greater intimacy with God, we will come to know him as our "interior Master of Christian prayer" (*CCC* 2672).

## The Holy Spirit in the Ministries and Charisms of the Church

We also discover the wind of the Spirit moving in those ministries and charisms that serve the mission of the Church. The Church does not have her own mission distinct from that of the Son and Spirit. The mission of the Church "is not an addition to that of Christ and the Holy Spirit, but is its sacrament" (*CCC* 738). Like a sacrament, the Church is the sign and instrument of the saving gift of Son and Spirit sent by the Father to draw humanity into communion with the Holy Trinity and with one another.

To fulfill this mission, the Holy Spirit imparts gifts to the Church. In order to better recognize the scope of the Spirit's presence in the Church, it will be helpful to highlight two ways in which the Spirit is working in the Church. The Spirit bestows both "hierarchic and charismatic gifts" and by these gifts guides and empowers the Church in fulfillment of her mission (*CCC* 768). "Hierarchic gifts" refer to the work of ordained ministry in the Church: bishops, priests, and deacons. "Charismatic gifts" refer to the working of the Spirit spread among all the faithful. Today, many understand the term "charismatic" too narrowly, associating the label only with certain charisms such as praying in tongues and healing. According to the witness of Scripture and Church teaching, however, these are but a few of innumerable charisms present in the Church. We will go into much more detail about such gifts and charisms of the Spirit in the next chapter. At this point, we simply want to highlight "hierarchical" and "charismatic" as describing two ways in which the Spirit is at work in the Church.

First it is important to emphasize that the Spirit works through the Church hierarchy of ordained ministry. Christ chose his apostles and breathed the Holy Spirit upon them, saying, "As the Father has sent me, so I send you....Receive the Holy Spirit. If you forgive the sins of any, they are forgiven them" (John 20:21–23). That gift of the Spirit is handed on to the bishops who succeed them.

To fulfill their exalted mission, the apostles were endowed by Christ with a special outpouring of the Holy Spirit coming upon them, and by the imposition of hands they passed on to their auxiliaries the gift of the Spirit, which is transmitted down to our day through episcopal consecration (*CCC* 1556).

The priests, too, receive a special anointing of the Spirit that configures them to Christ as priest, teacher, and shepherd of the flock entrusted to them (*CCC* 1563, 1585). Saint Paul spoke to the priests (presbyters) of the Church of Ephesus, saying, "The Holy Spirit has made you overseers, to shepherd the church of God (Acts 20:28).

The ordained ministries and the hierarchical structure of the Church that they provide are gifts of the Holy Spirit. The Church as a mystical body made up of many members is obviously much more extensive than the hierarchy, but that hierarchy gives structure to the body, much as our skeleton gives structure to our physical bodies. This structure fosters the visible unity of the body, the coordination of its many members and its continuity through time. We are sometimes tempted to set structure and Spirit in opposition and to view the Church hierarchy as a merely human institution resistant to the movement of the Spirit. Rather, that hierarchical, institutional structure is a gift of the Spirit to make the body of Christ visible in the world. The Church exists in an inseparable and mysterious unity of the visible and invisible, the human and the divine, hierarchical society and mystical body (*CCC* 779). While her human ministers often fail, the Spirit never fails to work through these weak human instruments to bring the word and sacraments of Christ to heal and strengthen us (*CCC* 1128–1129). We recognize and welcome the Spirit as we receive the gifts he brings to us through our shepherds in the Church.

The movement of the Spirit in the Church is not limited, how-ever, to the ordained and hierarchical ministry. The hierarchical gifts of the Spirit are complemented by the charismatic gifts poured out upon all the baptized. All of the faithful, through their baptism, receive their own share in the priesthood of Christ and are anointed by the Spirit to offer their lives in a spiritual sacrifice of praise to the Father (*CCC* 901). The Spirit gives special graces or charisms by which all the faithful share in the mission of the Church, carrying the truth of Christ into the world by their witness (*CCC* 798, 951). We will give many examples of such charisms in the next chapter.

The Spirit also inspires certain persons with a "personal charism," a particular vision of Christ and a specific way of follow-ing and serving him that they hand on to their followers as distinc-tive spiritualities or forms of religious life. Thus, for example, the personal charisms of Saint Francis, Saint Dominic, and Saint Igna-tius of Loyola are handed on as Franciscan, Dominican, and Ignati-an charisms inspiring and transforming the lives of their followers, whether in religious communities they founded or among all those who find inspiration in their witness, both among the ordained, the religious, and the laity. These charisms are received as special gifts of the Spirit animating and renewing the Church.

In order to fulfill their special responsibility to guide the faith-ful and to foster the unity of the flock, the bishops of the Church receive the charism of discerning charisms (*CCC* 801). By the spe-cial grace given to them as shepherds of the Church, the bishops confirm and foster authentic charisms and protect the flock from divisive and false spirits. Thus, the hierarchical and charismatic gifts complement one another for the good and harmony of the Church. This is not to deny that there may be moments of tension between bishops and charismatic saints. Many authentic saints, visionaries, and religious founders initially experienced opposition from the hierarchy. Given the need for careful discernment, it is not surprising that bishops tend toward caution in responding to claims of inspiration. The trial imposed upon the saint or visionary by this initial opposition and their patient and submissive endurance to the Church purifies and authenticates their vision. If the charism is authentic, the Church will confirm it—for the same Spirit who inspires the charism guides the hierarchy.

A story from the life of Saint Francis illustrates how the Spirit works through both hierarchical and charismatic gifts. Francis, a layman, was converted and inspired to a new form of religious life. He embraced the traditional elements of religious life, the vows of poverty, chastity, and obedience. But in his day, those vows would normally be lived within the stable life of a monastery. Saint Francis felt the Spirit prompting him to a life lived out among the people, begging for his daily bread in radical poverty and bringing the Gospel to the streets in radical imitation of Jesus Christ. Here the Holy Spirit was leading the Church, not through the deliberations of the bishops or through some program initiated and planned by the hierarchy but by the charism given to Francis. Yet, Francis knew that his vision, if genuinely given by the Spirit, required confirmation by the hierarchy. So he first placed himself under the care and protection of his bishop and then later carried his rule to Rome to be confirmed by the pope. One would not expect Pope Innocent III to confirm such a radical and novel transformation of religious life. Such an expectation, however, does not leave room for the movement of the Spirit. The Spirit spoke to the pope in a dream. In this dream, the pope saw the Church as a tottering building held up by one small man. The pope recognized Francis as the man from his dream. With the gift of discernment given by the Spirit, the pope confirmed the charism of Saint Francis, introducing a new form of religious life that brought renewal to the life of the Church and a source of continuing inspiration down through the ages.

We can also see that hierarchical discernment take a necessary disciplinary action in the history of the Franciscans. A later movement of so-called "Spiritual Franciscans" called the *Fraticelli,* gave Francis' teaching an elitist and divisive interpretation, which led to their suppression by the pope. The Holy Spirit guides the Church to confirm and support authentic movements that he has inspired and protects the flock from false movements. Within those movements inspired by the Spirit and confirmed by the hierarchy, we are invited to welcome the Spirit by receiving his gifts.

## The Holy Spirit in the Apostolic and Missionary Life of the Church

The Spirit inspires the evangelistic mission of the Church. The Holy Spirit makes the Church apostolic in two ways: sharing in apostolic truth and participating in the apostolic mission (*CCC* 863). The Spirit unites all members to the apostolic origin of the Church by communion with the faith received from Peter and the apostles and handed on by their successors, the popes and bishops. The gift of the Spirit ensures the authentic transmission and development of that truth and its reception by the faithful. The Spirit also gives all members a share in the apostolic mission of the Church. The apostolate, the mission of sharing Christ with the world, is given to every member of the Church. In our baptism, we come to share in the anointing of the Spirit to carry on the prophetic mission of Jesus in bringing the truth of God's saving grace to all peoples. The Church is by her very nature missionary because she originates in the mission of Son and Spirit and exists to bring all people into the communion of Father and Son in the Spirit (*CCC* 850). The Holy Spirit is the "protagonist, the principle agent" who leads the Church on a mission to the world (*CCC* 852). We welcome the Spirit and come to know him in intimacy as we open our hearts to share his desire, respond to his guidance, and yield to his energies as he leads us in sharing Christ with others.

## The Holy Spirit and the Saints

The Holy Spirit is given to make us holy. He is God's love poured into our hearts bringing forgiveness, healing the wounds of sin and granting us the power to love with the love of Christ (*CCC* 733–736). This gift of holiness is displayed in the lives of the saints. The catechism quotes Saint Basil's description of the light of the Spirit refracted through the saints:

> The Spirit is truly the dwelling of the saints and the saints are for the Spirit a place where he dwells as in his own home, since they offer themselves as a dwelling place for God and are called his temple (*CCC* 2684).

In one sense, all the members of the Church are called saints for the Church that has been made holy by Christ and has become the temple of the Holy Spirit (*CCC* 823). Yet, in the members of the Church, this holiness, while real, is still imperfect, and we are called to strive toward the perfection of love (*CCC* 825). We are called to become saints, not by our own unaided efforts but by our receptivity to the gift of the Holy Spirit. The Spirit unites us to Christ that we might die with Christ to our sin and selfishness and rise with Christ to a life of sacrificial love. To encourage our cooperation with the Spirit and teach us the Spirit's way of sanctification, the Church recognizes those who have manifested this holiness in their lives:

> By canonizing some of the faithful, that is by solemnly proclaiming that they practiced heroic virtue and lived in fidelity to God's grace, the Church recognizes the power of the Spirit of holiness within her and sustains the hope of believers by proposing the saints to them as models and intercessors (*CCC* 828).

The beauty of the Spirit is refracted in many ways by the diverse forms his gift of holiness assumes in the lives of the saints. We come to know the Holy Spirit by learning his ways as illustrated in the lives of the saints, by receiving his gifts mediated through the teachings of the saints, and by rejoicing in the communion the Holy Spirit forms between us and the saints as we rely on their intercession.

We, too, are called to become saints through the gifts the Holy Spirit gives us. We are called to join the saints in serving the Church through the charisms we receive from the Holy Spirit. Our next chapter will help us to understand and to receive these gifts and charisms.

## REFLECTION QUESTIONS

1. *How does the Holy Spirit work through the Scriptures to bring the word of God into our lives?*

2. *How does the Holy Spirit work through tradition and the magisterium to guide the Church?*

3. *What does the Holy Spirit do in the liturgy? How can we become more aware of and responsive to the Spirit's presence when we go to Mass?*

4. *How does the Spirit help us pray? How has the Spirit helped you pray?*

5. *How do hierarchical and charismatic gifts differ, and how do they work together?*

6. *Which saints have helped you know the Spirit better?*

# CHAPTER 4

# The Gifts, Fruits, and Charisms of the Spirit in Our Lives

## *A Variety of Gifts*

Saint Paul emphasizes the variety of gifts that the Holy Spirit distributed among all the members of the body of Christ (1 Corinthians 12:4). The one Holy Spirit, out of the generous bounty of "his own richness" and in order to meet the various needs within the Church "gives his different gifts for the welfare of the Church" (*CCC* 791). Within the unity of the Church there is at the same time a "great diversity" reflecting "both the variety of God's gifts and the diversity of those who receive them" (*CCC* 814). The Church is the body of Christ with many members, each receiving gifts for the mutual benefit of the other members and for the unity and enrichment of the whole body:

For just as the body is one and has many members, so it is with Christ. For in the one Spirit we were all baptized into one body...Indeed the body does not consist of one member but of many. If the foot would say, "Because I am not a hand, I do not belong to the body," that would not make it any less a part of the body. And if the ear would say, "Because I am not an eye, I do not belong to the body," that would not make it any less a part of the body. If the whole body were an eye, where would the hearing be? If the whole body were hearing, where would the sense of smell be? But as it is, God arranged the members in the body. There are many members, yet one body (1 Corinthians 12:12–20).

This diversity of gifts fosters our dependence upon one another and calls us to serve one another in a generous sharing of these gifts. The catechism explains that this diversity of gifts belongs to God's plan, "who wills that each receive what he needs from others, and that those endowed with particular 'talents' share the benefits with those who need them" (*CCC* 1937). The catechism illustrates this point by citing a message from God received by Saint Catherine of Siena:

I distribute the virtues quite diversely; I do not give all of them to each person, but some to one, some to others...I have given many gifts and graces, both spiritual and temporal, with such diversity that I have not given everything to one single person, so that you may be constrained to practice charity towards one another....I have willed that one should need another and that all should be my ministers in distributing the grace and gifts they have received from me (*CCC* 1937).

The great diversity of gifts poured out by the Holy Spirit calls us to give to others and receive from others, thus fostering our communion with one another in the body of Christ. This diversity of gifts also adds to the richness and beauty of the body of Christ. In his third-century work, *On the Trinity*, Novatian describes the gifts that the Spirit distributes as the ornaments of the Church given her by Christ, her spouse. These many and varied gifts of the Holy Spirit are like many beautiful jewels adorning the Church, the beloved bride of Christ who through these many gifts prepares herself for Christ, her bridegroom.

The Holy Spirit is one, but his gifts are many. To help us understand and describe the many gifts of the Spirit, it is helpful to categorize them. The first helpful distinction is between those gifts of the Holy Spirit given to us for our own growth in holiness and those gifts of the Holy Spirit given through us to benefit others through our service. We may call the first group the sanctifying gifts of the Holy Spirit (the seven gifts) and the second are best described by the New Testament term, "charisms." The word "charism" simply means "graces" or "gifts of grace." The word is associated today with the charismatic movement and such charismatic gifts as praying in tongues and healing, but as we will see below when we discuss this term in more detail, there are many charismatic gifts that encompass both ordinary and extraordinary graces. Before considering charisms in more detail, we will first describe the seven sanctifying gifts of the Spirit and the fruit of the Spirit. Then we will clarify the distinction between those gifts and the charisms before proceeding onto the innumerable charisms of the Spirit.

## The Sanctifying Gifts of the Holy Spirit

The seven sanctifying gifts of the Holy Spirit are given to complete and perfect our growth in virtue. To understand these gifts it is helpful to review the role of virtues in our growth in grace. The goal of the virtuous life is to become like God (*CCC* 1803). Virtues are habitual dispositions to do what is good. The virtues of faith, hope, and love are known as the theological virtues because they have their origin and their goal in God (*theos*). These three virtues originate in God's gift. They are infused in the soul by the gift of God's grace given in baptism. Their goal is our union with God. By faith and hope in God we are empowered by the Holy Spirit to unite ourselves to God in love. Our growth in love comes through the practice of the cardinal human virtues of prudence, justice, fortitude, and temperance through continued human effort empowered and elevated by divine grace. The Holy Spirit is already present and at work in our practice of these virtues. Wounded by sin, we can achieve growth in virtue only by the healing and help provided by the Holy Spirit.

While the Holy Spirit is present and working through our acquisition and growth in virtue, the assistance of the Spirit goes even further. The practice of virtue is further perfected by the gifts of the Holy Spirit. The practice of the virtues can be compared to rowing a boat. We are pulling on the oars, receiving strength and direction from the Holy Spirit. The more we pull on the oars in time with the Spirit, the more we build our spiritual muscles and become more and more proficient in the practice of virtue. With the gifts of the Spirit, we are given sails for the boat and receive the capacity to be carried by the power of the Holy Spirit to greater heights of holiness beyond our human capacity. The gifts of the Holy Spirit raise human virtues to a divine level. For example, we may compare the virtue of fortitude with the gift of fortitude. The virtue of fortitude is a habit of perseverance and constancy in doing good, developed by repeated effort empowered by grace. The gift of fortitude is a receptivity that enables one to be lifted by the power of the Spirit to a God-like fortitude that remains committed to God even in the face of great difficulties and suffering. The virtue of fortitude prepared the martyrs to face death for their faith; the gift of fortitude empowered them to face that death with peace and joy.

John Paul II gives a concise, illuminating, and inspiring catechesis on the seven gifts of the Holy Spirit in one of his general audiences (4/3/1991). John Paul defines the gifts as "exquisitely divine energies which the Holy Spirit pours into the soul." These divine energies perfect the virtues by giving the human spirit the capacity to act in a divine way. Every Christian receives these gifts according to the generous measure of God's love accommodated to their vocation and their specific individual spiritual journey. The seven gifts correspond to the basic dynamism of the spiritual life: gifts of wisdom, knowledge, and understanding to illuminate the mind; gifts of counsel and fortitude to strengthen the decisions of the will; and gifts of piety and reverence that enable us to grow in a personal relationship to God through prayer and an upright life. John Paul II summarizes the individual gifts as follows: the gift of wisdom enlightens the intellect for spiritual understanding, helping the Christian to understand reality from a divine perspective. The gift of understanding gives insight and interior understanding of God's word. The gift of knowledge is a supernatural capacity to grasp the content of divine revelation and to discern the things of God in one's knowledge of the world. The gift of counsel is a supernatural ability to regulate one's life and choices, no matter how difficult, in accord with the guidance of the Holy Spirit. The gift of fortitude supports the will in prompt and persevering faithfulness to God's commands in the face of great difficulties, even to the point of martyrdom, not only dying for the Faith, but also the more common martyrdom of illness and infirmity. (John Paul would later illustrate these words by his own heroic witness of fortitude as he endured illness at the end of his life.) With the gift of piety, the Holy Spirit "directs the heart of man toward God with feelings, affections, thoughts, and prayers" that express our relation to the Father as his children in Jesus Christ, as well as our relation to Christ, Mary, and the saints. The seventh gift of the Holy Spirit, the fear of the Lord, fills the soul with a profound respect for God's law. It is not a servile fear but a "filial fear steeped in love." The fear of the Lord is a profound reverence toward God, who has so lovingly adopted us as his children. John Paul II concludes his catechesis on the gifts of the Spirit with an exhortation to be "in tune" with the Holy Spirit, whose love is manifested by his many gifts.

## The Fruits of the Holy Spirit

Our response to the seven gifts of the Holy Spirit produces in us the fruits of the Spirit. The catechism describes these fruits as "perfections that the Holy Spirit forms in us" and lists them as "charity, joy, peace, patience, kindness, goodness, generosity, gentleness, faithfulness, modesty, self-control, and chastity" (CCC 1832, Galatians 5:22–23). These fruits describe the result of the grace of the Holy Spirit at work in us. When we respond to the Spirit, these are the fruits that blossom in our lives. By the power of the Spirit, we are grafted into Christ the vine and bear the fruit of Christ-likeness (CCC 736). United to Christ by the Holy Spirit, the members of his Church become the budding forth of the kingdom of God in the present world. Saint Paul succinctly describes this kingdom as "righteousness and peace and joy in the Holy Spirit" (Romans 14:17). The Holy Spirit works in us to produce these fruits of holiness working through word and sacrament, through virtues and gifts, through the apostolic ministry of his ordained ministers and "by the many special graces (called charisms), by which he makes the faithful fit and ready to undertake various tasks and offices for the renewal and building up of the Church" (*CCC* 798).

## The Difference Between the Seven Gifts of the Holy Spirit and Charisms

In our preparation for confirmation, we learn about the seven gifts of the Holy Spirit: wisdom, understanding, counsel, fortitude, knowledge, piety, and fear of the Lord. This list comes from an Old Testament prophecy about the Spirit's anointing upon the Messiah:

> The Spirit of the Lord shall rest on him, the spirit of wisdom and understanding, the spirit of counsel and might, the spirit of knowledge and the fear of the LORD. His delight shall be in the fear of the LORD (Isaiah 11:2–3).

The twofold repetition of "fear of the Lord" in modern translations was rendered in the ancient Greek and Latin translations of the Old Testament, first as "piety" and second as "fear of the Lord," and that is how the Church Fathers came up with our traditional list of seven gifts. Anointed by the Spirit at his baptism, Jesus the Messiah received these gifts from the Spirit in order to share them with us. Through baptism we are called to share in Christ's mission as his disciples, and through confirmation we are anointed by the Spirit, receiving an increase of his gifts that we might become more Christlike. These gifts are given to complete and perfect our practice of virtue by making us receptive to the promptings of the Holy Spirit toward holy living (*CCC* 1830–31).

In addition to these seven gifts listed by Isaiah, we find several lists of gifts in the writings of Saint Paul. These gifts (*charismata* in the Greek language) contain such gifts as knowledge, wisdom, prophecy, healing, miracles, praying in tongues, discernment of spirits, giving, teaching, exhorting, and many others. The catechism defines these charisms as "special graces" that the Spirit gives, not for our justification and sanctification but in order to associate us with his work, allowing us to collaborate in the salvation of others and in the growth of the Church (*CCC* 2003). Charisms are gifts in which the Holy Spirit works through us to bring God's blessings to others.

Saint Thomas Aquinas distinguishes between the sanctifying gifts of the Spirit and charisms as two types of grace (*Summa Theologica* I.II. Question 111). The sanctifying gifts are part of the grace of justification that Saint Thomas describes in Latin as *Gratia gratum faciens,* which could be translated as "grace which makes pleasing." The seven gifts of the Holy Spirit are given to make us pleasing to God by transforming us more and more into the image of Christ. They belong to the grace of justification that makes us holy. Saint Thomas describes the charisms in Latin as *gratiae gratis datae,* which can be translated as "gratuitous gifts." Saint Thomas admits that the sanctifying gifts are also given gratuitously, but they are named for their common end: to make us pleasing to God by our sanctification. The charisms, by contrast, serve multiple ends, reflecting their great variety. What they have in common is their gratuitous source in the generosity of the Holy Spirit. The Holy Spirit generously pours out gifts upon the members of the Church and just as generously allows us to participate in his work by giving those gifts through us to bless others. As examples of charisms or gratuitous graces, Saint Thomas lists: prophecy, rapture, tongues, words of wisdom and knowledge, and miracles. Saint Thomas discusses the seven sanctifying gifts of the Holy Spirit in relation to virtues and growth in holiness (*Summa Theologica* I.II, Question 68), and he discusses the charisms in relation to the variety of Christian states of life (*Summa Theologica* I.II, Questions 171–178). Similarly, the seven gifts of the Holy Spirit are described in the third part of the catechism, which focuses on Christian morality (*CCC* 1830–1831). The charisms are discussed in the section on the mission of the Church in the first part of the catechism (*CCC* 799–801).

## Charisms

To better understand charisms, it is helpful to begin with the vocabulary of Scripture. The New Testament uses a variety of terms for these gifts. Most important are the Greek words *charisma* (singular) and *charismata* (plural), rendered as "charism" in English. This word is extremely rare in the Greek language, and never with the precise meaning found in the New Testament, leading many biblical scholars to suspect that Saint Paul may have coined the term. The root of the word is *charis* (grace), and the word "charism" is used to describe the multiple ways in which God's grace is at work and manifested through God's people. Perhaps Saint Paul simply made this word up to describe the many ways in which he observed the grace of God working in the Church. The term can sometimes be used in a general way for such blessings as eternal life (Romans 6:23), God's gifts (Romans 11:29), or specific answers to prayer (2 Corinthians 1:11). But most frequently, Saint Paul uses the term to describe the many specific gifts of grace given to God's people by which they minister to one another. (1 Corinthians 12:4, 9, 28, 30;

Romans 12:6 and others). The meaning of the term is illustrated by Saint Paul's description of them as "gifts (charisms) that differ according to the grace (*charis*) given to us" (Romans 12:6). The grace given to the whole Church and to each Christian is manifested in manifold and different ways as concrete expressions of graceful gifts given from one member of the Church to another for the mutual benefit and up-building of the whole Church.

Saint Paul links charism with another term when he speaks of his desire to impart a "spiritual gift" to strengthen the Christians in Rome (Romans 1:11). "Spiritual gifts" in this verse translates the Greek phrase *charism pneumatikon. Pneumatikon* is taken from the Greek word for Spirit (*pneuma*) and is used to describe spiritual gifts, persons, or powers. Saint Paul uses the word "spiritual" to describe charisms as works of the Holy Spirit.

Another term by which Saint Paul related these gifts to the Holy Spirit was the Greek word *phanerosis,* translated in English as "manifestation." In 1 Corinthians 12:7, Saint Paul says, "to each is given the manifestation of the Spirit for the common good." Later in that letter he describes how these manifestations lead those who witness them to declare "God is really among you" (1 Corinthians 14:25). These gifts are the manifestation of the presence of the Holy Spirit at work in the midst of the Church. Through these gifts, others recognize the presence of God as it is manifested in and through his people. The invisible presence of the Holy Spirit is manifested through his gifts.

While Saint Paul frequently associates charisms with the Holy Spirit, he uses Trinitarian language to fully describe these manifestations of grace. Saint Paul associates these gifts with the Spirit, the Son, and the Father:

Now there are varieties of gifts but the same Spirit; and there
are varieties of services, but the same Lord; and there are
varieties of activities, but it is the same God who activates all
of them (1 Corinthians 12:4–6).

Saint Paul begins with the common vocabulary by referring to
the variety of gifts (*charismata*) of the Holy Spirit. Despite the variety of gifts, they are the work of one Holy Spirit. Then Saint Paul
refers to Jesus Christ by his common title of "Lord" and refers to
these gifts as varied services or ministries of the one Lord. Saint
Paul uses the Greek word (*diakinoia*), often translated as "service"
or "ministry," which is also related to the title of "deacon." Here he
refers to these gifts as services or ministries of the Lord Jesus Christ.
Through these gifts, Jesus Christ exercises his ministry or his service, working through the members of his body. So for example,
when a Christian exercises a charism of healing and through prayer
and the gift of the Holy Spirit someone receives healing, that is the
healing ministry of Jesus Christ working through his Church. The
members of the Church receive gifts of the Holy Spirit to equip them
to share in the ongoing ministry of Jesus Christ through his Church.
This ministry of Jesus Christ is also the work of God the Father.
Saint Paul refers to these charisms of the Spirit, or these services of
the Lord, as also the activities of God. The Greek word translated as
activities is *energemata*. The energy of God, his work of redeeming
creation, is performed through the ministry of his Son, our Lord
Jesus Christ continuing in the Church through the outpouring of
gifts from the Holy Spirit. So, we may refer to these gifts as charisms
of the Spirit or ministries of the Lord Jesus, or activities of God the
Father. The variety of gifts finds their unity in the unity of the Holy
Trinity present and active within the Church.

In addition to the various terms already described, sometimes Scripture refers to these charisms by the simple term "gift." Using the simple Greek term for gift (*doma*), Saint Paul speaks of the ascended Lord who gave "gifts" to his people (Ephesians 4:7). This term in a quite simple way conveys the fact that all of these gifts are like "presents." They originate in the generous love of God, who pours out a rich multiplicity of gifts upon his people through the original gift and giver, the Holy Spirit.

Saint Paul also describes charisms as "activated" by the Spirit (1 Corinthians 12:6, 11). The Spirit activates these gifts through his inspirations in our soul. John Paul II describes these inspirations as "promptings of grace" (*On the Vocation and Mission of the Lay Faithful: Christifidelis Laici,* 24). The catechism also describes charisms as "promptings" of the Holy Spirit (*CCC* 800). Charisms are experienced as promptings of grace, an interior call from the Spirit who generously invites us to share in his work within the Church and the world. That call may be experienced as something surprising and unexpected as the Spirit in his freedom calls those he wishes and makes them capable of fulfilling the task to which he calls them. Other times, that call may seem quite ordinary, as when someone becomes aware of needs within the Church and offers his or her time and talents to meet those needs, scarcely aware that this is a response to a prompting of the Holy Spirit offered in this charism of service.

While the charisms can be experienced as a personal call and invitation from the Spirit, such promptings are not to be taken in an individualistic manner without reference to the Church and its leadership. The charisms are intended by the Holy Spirit for the good of the whole Church, whom that same Spirit holds in unity. Saint Paul warns the Thessalonian Church against quenching the Spirit but at the same time calls them to "test everything" (1 Thessalonians 5:19–21). The Spirit equips the pastors of the Church with gifts of discernment that they may confirm and direct the charisms according to the needs of the whole Church. Therefore, the catechism emphasizes:

> Discernment of charisms is always necessary. No charism is exempt from being referred and submitted to the Church's shepherds. Their office is…to test all things…so that all the diverse and complementary charisms work together for the common good (*CCC* 801).

## Charisms in Scripture

After exploring the biblical vocabulary for charisms, it is helpful to review the various lists of charisms found in the New Testament. 1 Corinthians 12:8–10 lists wisdom, knowledge, faith, healing, miracles, prophecy, discernment of spirits, tongues, and interpretation of tongues. 1 Corinthians 12:28 lists apostles, prophets, teachers, miracles, healing, assistance, leadership, and tongues. Romans 12:6–8 lists prophecy, ministry, teaching, exhortation, giving, leadership, and acts of compassion. Ephesians 4:11 lists apostles, prophets, evangelists, pastors, and teachers. 1 Peter 4:10–11 refers simply to those who speak and those who serve. One should notice a number of things about these lists. First, while some gifts appear multiple times, none of these lists are the same. Each list contains some examples of the great variety of gifts found within the Church. Saint Paul wishes to emphasize that there is a great variety of gifts distributed by the Holy Spirit according to his will, and these gifts should not be the occasion for jealousy, pride, discord, or division. There is a great diversity of gifts, but all are from the same Holy Spirit who gives his gifts to foster the unity of the body. Secondly, one should notice that charisms may describe specific and concrete manifestations or occurrences such as a word of wisdom or a healing; they may describe ongoing ministries or activities such as teaching or administration; or they may describe offices such as apostles or prophets. The use of the term "charism" seems fluid in Saint Paul's vocabulary. So, for example, a charism of teaching could describe one instance of inspired teaching, or an ongoing ministry of teaching or a person having an office as teacher in the Church. In each case, there is a manifestation of the Spirit working through a member of the body of Christ to bring some blessing to others. Finally, among the diversity of gifts listed one should notice that there are those we might think more extraordinary and supernatural such as miracles and healings and those we might think of us as more ordinary such as teaching, administration, giving, and acts of mercy. All of these are considered charisms in the New Testament. We often make the mistake today of limiting charismatic gifts to such things as healing and praying in tongues, whereas Saint Paul also lists giving, acts of mercy, administration, teaching, and many other seemingly ordinary activities as charismatic gifts.

## Ordinary Charisms

The catechism also speaks of the fact that the charisms include both ordinary and extraordinary graces:

> Whether extraordinary or simple and humble, charisms are graces of the Holy Spirit that directly or indirectly benefit the Church…Whatever their character—sometimes it is extraordinary, such as the gift of miracles or of tongues

—charisms are oriented toward sanctifying grace and are intended for the common good of the Church (CCC 799, 2003).

In one sense, no gift of the Spirit is truly "ordinary" but, in contrast to those charisms that seem (to us) more extraordinary we may describe these simple and humble gifts as "ordinary" charisms. Saint Peter seems to describe the more ordinary charisms when he writes simply of the charisms exercised by those who speak and those who serve. In this exhortation, Saint Peter describes how ordinary human activities of speaking and serving may be elevated by the action of the Holy Spirit into charismatic gifts:

> Like good stewards of the manifold grace of God, serve one another with whatever gift [charism] each of you has received. Whoever speaks must do so as one speaking the very words of God; whoever serves must do so with the strength that God supplies (1 Peter 4:10–11).

Saint Peter begins by reminding his readers that each one has received gifts (charisms) as stewards of God's grace, which they are given in order to serve others. He then urges them to take their human abilities, the ability to speak or the ability to serve, and to exercise those abilities under the inspiration and in the strength that the Holy Spirit provides. Those who speak are to allow the Holy Spirit to inspire them so they speak God's message. Those who serve are to serve not in their own limited human abilities but in the power and assistance provided by the Holy Spirit. Human talents or abilities elevated by grace, led and empowered by the Holy Spirit, become charisms, gifts of the Holy Spirit that bring God's blessing to others. Since all of these gifts are exercised in the power that comes from

God, the final result, according to Saint Peter, is that it is God who is glorified as the source of these gifts.

As an example of this, we may consider the charism of teaching. Someone already has the ability to speak before a classroom, some understanding of the faith, at least some aptitude for teaching, and he or she senses a prompting of the Spirit to volunteer to teach in the parish religious education program. That prompting may have come from a phone call from the director of religious education or a bulletin announcement asking for volunteers, but whatever the external source, there is an interior thought, no matter how slight, that this invitation may come from the Holy Spirit. The new volunteer studies and prepares and does his or her best to present the lesson with a prayer for the assistance of the Holy Spirit. As the teacher sees the young minds of the students illuminated with a grasp of the faith that moves their minds and hearts toward God, the teacher may recognize that the Holy Spirit has worked through him or her in a way surpassing human ability. The Holy Spirit has conveyed God's truth as a living reality through the charism of teaching. Another person might be moved out of concern for the poor to volunteer for some work of mercy. As he experiences God's power working through him to bring God's blessing to others, he becomes aware that his service is a charism, a manifestation of the power of the Spirit at work.

In his teaching on charisms, Pope John Paul II emphasizes that the lists found in the New Testament are not exhaustive but simply indicate representative gifts significant in the Church at that time. John Paul teaches that the Holy Spirit continues to give new charisms in response to new needs in the history of the Church. As contemporary examples of charisms in the Church today, John Paul mentions working with the poor, the sick, or the disabled; giving spiritual direction and counseling; and inspired preaching, teaching, or writing. He gives these as just a few examples of the "enormous range of charisms" given by the Holy Spirit (2/27/1991).

## Charisms of Ministry and Vocation

As can be seen in the lists from the New Testament, many charisms are associated with offices and ministries in the Church. Saint Paul refers to apostles, teachers, evangelists, pastors, and prophets as Christ's gifts to the Church. Ministry activities such as administration, teaching, and service are listed as charisms. The catechism refers to these as "graces of state that accompany the exercise of responsibilities of the Christian life and of the ministries within the Church" (*CCC* 2004).

There are charisms that accompany the grace of holy orders. Saint Paul recalled the ordination of Saint Timothy and encouraged him to "rekindle the gift (charism) of God that is within you through the laying on of my hands" (2 Timothy 1:6). The catechism mentions the charism of truth and infallibility, which is given to the pope and the bishops as shepherds of the Church so that they might fulfill the ministry given to them by Christ, to teach the people of God and guide them into all truth (*CCC* 94, 890). When the pope or the bishops united as a whole with the pope proclaim a truth of faith or morals in a definitive way, it is through a special charism of the Holy Spirit that they are able to do so with infallibility. The Spirit gives them these gifts for the benefit of the whole Church. Not only the pope and bishops, but all ministries in the Church receive charisms. By these many charisms the Holy Spirit makes the faithful "fit and ready to undertake various tasks and offices for the renewal and building up of the Church" (*CCC* 798). John Paul II emphasizes that hierarchy and charism are not in conflict. The offices or ordained ministries of the Church are themselves gifts or charisms of the Spirit given for the good of the whole Church. There are charisms given with each office in the Church, including the charism of Peter given to the pope as well as charisms for bishops, priests, and deacons (2/27/1991).

However, it is not only ordained ministry who receive charisms, but lay ministry, also. The catechism clearly teaches this:

> The laity can also feel called, or be in fact called, to cooperate with their pastors in the service of the ecclesial community, for the sake of its growth and life. This can be done through the exercise of different kinds of ministries according to the grace and charisms which the Lord has been pleased to bestow on them (*CCC* 910).

John Paul II listed many lay ministries as examples of charisms, including lectors, acolytes, extraordinary eucharistic ministers, catechists, and religion teachers in schools, those who assist with music and liturgy, those who lead Bible studies, those who direct charitable works, and others who serve the Church as administrators (8/5/1991). All such tasks, when undertaken in response to the prompting of the Holy Spirit and performed with his assistance and under his direction with an attitude of humble self-giving, may become charisms, gifts of the Spirit bringing divine blessings to others and building up the Church.

Consecrated life is also described as a charism (*CCC* 1175). Those called to religious life and those called to celibate priesthood embrace continence for the kingdom of God as a charism of the Holy Spirit. In his First Letter to the Corinthians, Saint Paul extolled the values of a celibate life for undivided devotion to the Lord (1 Corinthians 7:32–35) and expressed his wish that all could be celibate like him, but qualified that wish by recognizing that "each has a particular gift (charism) from God" (1 Corinthians 7:7). Based on Saint Paul, John Paul II, in his *Theology of the Body,* describes continence for the sake of the kingdom as a charismatic orientation, a charismatic choice, and a charismatic sign (*Man and Woman He Created Them: A Theology of the Body*, §73, 75). People who receive this gift of the Spirit respond to a call to orient their lives toward the heavenly goal of union with God, receiving grace to choose that life in joyful surrender and by the power of the Spirit, live their lives as anticipatory signs of spousal union with God in heaven.

Just as celibacy for the kingdom is a charism, so, too, is marriage. Saint Paul wrote, "each has a particular gift (charism) from God, one having one kind and another a different kind" (1 Corinthians 7:7). As John Paul II explains this passage, both those called to celibacy and those called to marriage receive a true gift from God, a charism or grace that empowers them to live their vocation. Therefore, marriage is both "sacramental and charismatic." Through this charism of the Spirit, marriage provides a way of living in the body as a temple of the Holy Spirit. Through this charism of marriage, the couple is empowered by the Spirit to master the pull of concupiscence and to experience the freedom of self-giving to one another in spousal love and communion, open to the gift of life. John Paul II interprets the mutual "reverence" to which husband and wife are called in the book of Ephesians as a charismatic gift of the Holy Spirit. If they collaborate with this gift, the Holy Spirit will fill the couple with a reverence toward the mystery of their marriage as sacred sign, reverence toward one another as persons, and reverence for the unitive and life-giving power of their spousal union. Marriage is a charismatic vocation to be lived through the power of the gifts of the Holy Spirit. (*Man and Woman He Created Them: A Theology of the Body*, § 84, 85, 101, 117b, 131).

## Extraordinary Charisms

In addition to the ordinary charisms in which the Holy Spirit inspires, empowers, and works through our human talents and abilities, there are also more extraordinary charisms in which the Holy Spirit provides supernatural powers beyond natural human abilities to manifest his presence through miraculous signs. As noted above, the Catholic Church affirms both the ordinary charisms and the more extraordinary. A few specific examples of the more extraordinary charisms found within the Church include praying in tongues, miracles, and healing (*CCC* 2003, 1508). Saint Paul provides a representative list of miraculous charisms in 1 Corinthians 12:

> To each is given the manifestation of the Spirit for the common good. To one is given through the Spirit the utterance of wisdom, and to another the utterance of knowledge according to the same Spirit, to another faith by the same Spirit, to another gifts of healing by the one Spirit, to another the working of miracles, to another prophecy, to another the discernment of spirits, to another various kinds of tongues, to another the interpretation of tongues (1 Corinthians 12:7–10).

This list of nine gifts may be categorized as gifts of miraculous insight, speech, and power.

Gifts of inspired insight and understanding include knowledge, wisdom, and discernment of spirits. By the charism of knowledge, one comes to know something through an interior illumination of the mind by the Spirit. Saint Padre Pio experienced this charism, often knowing the sins of those who came to him for confession by supernatural knowledge. The charism of wisdom is an experience of divine guidance, an inspired sense of direction by which one comes to understand a plan or situation from the perspective of divine wisdom. The discernment of spirits grants an intuitive understanding of the presence or activity of spiritual power, whether that be the Spirit of God, angelic spirits, or demonic spirits.

Gifts of inspired insight also include knowledge given through inspired dreams and visions. Saint Peter proclaimed that through the gift of the Holy Spirit poured out on the Church, the prophecy of Joel would be fulfilled in the Church by an outpouring of dreams and visions to both young and old (Acts 2:17). From the pages of Scripture, through the writings of the Fathers, in the lives of medieval mystics and saints, down to twentieth-century visionaries such as Saint Faustina, the history of the Catholic Church is replete with visions, dreams, and apparitions. The Church is open to the reality that God continues to speak to his people in such ways. Yet, the Church very carefully distinguishes between these "private revelations" and the public revelation given in its fullness by the coming of Christ. These private revelations are not intended to surpass or correct the fullness of divine revelation given in Christ, and they must be judged in light of that revelation as it is understood and handed on by the magisterium. These charisms of inspired vision and knowledge are given to help us more fully and faithfully respond to the fullness of the revelation of God in Christ (*CCC* 67).

Gifts of speech include prophecy, tongues, and interpretation of tongues. The charism of prophecy is inspired speech that communicates divine truth. While prophecy may include prediction of future events, the emphasis of Christian prophecy is less fore-telling and more forth-telling. Saint Paul describes the gift of prophecy as Spirit-inspired words of "building up and encouragement and consolation" (1 Corinthians 14:3). Spirit-inspired preaching and teaching can become a charism of prophecy when it conveys God's message with spiritual power. The charism of prophecy is more evident when it conveys a message from the Lord such as we find in the writings of such visionaries as Saint Catherine of Siena or Saint Faustina. They deliver prophetic messages from the Lord that bring us encouragement and consolation.

We should not think of this gift as limited to such saints, however. As we pray for others, we may receive a word of encouragement or consolation that the Lord would like us to share with them. We can simply say, "As I was praying for you I felt like the Lord was saying...." If that word brings them consolation or encouragement, we will have some indication that it was an authentic word of prophecy. There is, of course, some danger of subjectivity, and we must learn to use these charisms with prudence and discernment. Saint Paul exhorts the Church, "Do not quench the Spirit. Do not despise the words of prophets, but test everything; hold fast to what is good" (1 Thessalonians 5:19–21).

Praying in tongues is inspired prayer in a language unknown and unlearned by the speaker, or inspired language-like words and sounds uttered in praise to God. This prayer may be accompanied by the gift of interpretation by which one comes to understand the meaning of the prayer. The apostles, gathered in the upper room praying for the sending of the Spirit on the day of Pentecost, began to pray in other tongues as they were moved by the Spirit (Acts 2:4). To many of the outsiders gathered there, it sounded like drunken gibberish. They mocked the apostles saying, "they are filled with new wine." To which, Peter replied, "it is only nine o'clock in the morning," that is, too early for drunkenness! But others, who had traveled from many lands in pilgrimage to Jerusalem, heard the apostles praising God in the languages of their native lands (Acts 2:5–15). Praying in tongues accompanied other subsequent outpourings of the Holy Spirit described in the Book of Acts: As Peter was preaching to the gentiles gathered at the house of Cornelius, the Spirit was poured out and those gentiles began praying in tongues (Acts 10:46); when Saint Paul baptized and laid hands on some disciples in Ephesus, the Holy Spirit came upon them and they spoke in tongues and prophesied (Acts 19:6). Even though Saint Paul chided the Corinthians for overemphasizing tongues over other spiritual gifts, he nonetheless told them, "I thank God that I speak in tongues more than all of you" (1 Corinthians 14:18). Saint Paul describes praying in tongues as praying with the spirit in contrast to praying with the mind and concludes that he will do both. He will sing and pray with his spirit, and he will sing and pray with his mind (1 Corinthians 14:15). Based on this description and contemporary experience of this charism, praying in tongues can be understood as a way of praying that surpasses the limitations of discursive prayer and gives full expression to the emotions of adoration and praise for God. Some have seen a reference to praying in tongues in patristic accounts of "jubilation." Saint Augustine for example, wrote in his exposition of Psalm 32, "What is it to sing in jubilation?....It is to be unable to explain in words what is sung by the heart...to exult with joy in the words of a song...to be filled with so great a joy that they cannot set it forth with words and turn away from the syllables of words to pass to the sound of jubilation." Praying in tongues is one way in which the Holy Spirit "helps us in our weakness; for we do not know how to pray as we ought, but that very Spirit intercedes with sighs too deep for words" (Romans 8:26).

This charism frequently accompanied the gift of the Spirit in the early history of the Church as we see reflected in the Book of Acts and in 1 Corinthians. Saint Irenaeus and Novatian mention this charism among those existing in the Church of the second and third centuries. The gift seems to have become less prevalent as time went on, however. Even though he may have experienced this charism in the experience of jubilation, Saint Augustine commented on the fact that the sign of tongues no longer accompanied the giving of the Spirit in baptism as it did in the early days of the Church. He explained this (in his commentary on the Gospel of John) by interpreting the Pentecost gift of tongues as a sign of the future catholicity of the Church. Now, spread throughout the world, the Catholic Church speaks in all tongues (languages) of the nations.

In more recent times, with the advent of the charismatic renewal movement in the Catholic Church, many Catholics testify to receiving this charism, and it frequently accompanies their experience of a fresh infilling of the Holy Spirit. This fresh infilling or baptism of the Spirit is understood within the Catholic charismatic renewal as an experiential renewal of the gift of the Holy Spirit given in baptism and confirmation. For many in this renewal, this experience has been accompanied by the charism of praying in tongues, and that charism has provided something of a breakthrough to a greater docility to the Holy Spirit and openness to many other charisms. Perhaps God is pouring out this gift in abundance today in answer to our rationalistic suspicion of the supernatural and in response to our need for this gift to help us pray. All are encouraged to pray for a fresh experience of the Holy Spirit open to this charism, but it is up to the Spirit to grant whichever charisms he chooses to give. The Catholic Church agrees with Pentecostals that the gift of tongues is a charism given to Christians today (*CCC* 2003) but disagrees with those who insist that it is a gift intended for every single Christian. Saint Paul himself was clear that not all speak in tongues, and it is the Holy Spirit who distributes his gifts as he wills (1 Corinthians 12:11, 29–30; *CCC* 951).

In addition to these gifts of knowledge and speech, the Holy Spirit also grants charisms of power. The charism of faith is not identical with the theological virtue of faith, but is a special grace by which one receives faith to pray for miracles. Saint Thérèse of Lisieux exemplified this charism of faith when she prayed with great confidence for the conversion of a notorious condemned criminal who had refused every opportunity to repent and confess his sins before his execution. Her prayers were answered, and she was assured that her prayer had been heard when she read in the newspaper how the condemned man kissed the crucifix before going to his death. This gift of faith also receives manifestations of divine power through charisms of miracles and healings. These are the signs and wonders that accompany the proclamation of the Gospel. Christ continues his healing ministry through the Church. He does so through the sacrament of the anointing of the sick, through the many doctors and nurses who work in Catholic hospitals, but also through the charism of healing through prayer that is given to some (*CCC* 1508).

Some would restrict the miraculous charisms to the early Church. Some have taught that the miraculous charisms ceased with the end of the apostolic age, but that teaching is not supported by Scripture or the evidence of history. Saint Paul says that the charisms will persist in the Church until the "perfect comes" when we see God "face to face" and we know fully what we only know now in part (1 Corinthians 13:8–12). These miraculous charisms will remain in the Church until Christ comes again in glory at the final judgment.

The early Church Fathers provide many witnesses to the continuing presence of miraculous gifts within the Church. Writing in the second century, Saint Irenaeus witnessed the following charisms in the Church of his day: casting out demons, prophetic foreknowledge, visions, prophetic utterances, speaking in tongues, healing of the sick, and even raising the dead. He said it was impossible to count the number of charisms given to the Church. In his third-century work on the Trinity, Novatian described the following charisms distributed in the Church by the Spirit: prophecy, teaching, speaking in tongues, healings, discernment of spirits, administration, and counsel. In the fourth century, Saint Cyril of Jerusalem continues to find these miraculous charisms in the Church of his day and adds to them the charisms of religious life, vowed poverty and chastity, which had emerged in the Church. In his catechetical lectures, Saint Cyril lists the following as charisms: wisdom, prophecy, casting out demons, interpretation of Scripture, alms-giving, fasting, chastity, and poverty. In the fourth-century version of the Rite of Christian Initiation for Adults (RCIA), Saint Cyril of Jerusalem taught candidates for baptism to prepare their souls to receive "heavenly gifts" such as "prophecy" and other charisms of the Spirit.

As we move from the first centuries into the later patristic era and on into the Middle Ages, the charisms seem to become less prevalent and no longer widely expected as a normal part of Christian life. Nonetheless, the charisms do not disappear from Catholic life. These charisms appear again and again in the lives of the saints. We find gifts of divine wisdom and prophecy, miraculous healings, visions, discernment of spirits, and other charisms appearing in the lives of the saints. While charisms remained as part of Catholic faith, associated with many saints down through the ages, the biblical and early patristic understanding of the wider role of charisms in the life of the Church was largely forgotten.

The Second Vatican Council restored "charisms" to their place within the Church. Blessed Pope John XXIII began the second Vatican Council of the 1960s by praying, "renew your wonders in our time as through a new Pentecost!" As the bishops worked on the Vatican II Constitution on the Church, there was debate over the role of charisms in the Church. Leon-Joseph Cardinal Suenens called for a clearer articulation of the biblical teaching that charisms are given to every Christian. As a result, the Vatican II Constitution on the Church (*Lumen Gentium*) clearly taught that the Holy Spirit distributes his charisms to all of the faithful.

> Moreover, it is not only through the sacraments and the ministries that the Holy Spirit makes the people holy, leads them and enriches them with his virtues. Allotting his gifts at will to each individual (1 Corinthians 12:11), he also distributes special graces among the faithful of every rank. By these gifts, he makes them fit and ready to undertake various tasks and offices for the renewal and building-up of the Church, as it is written, "To each is given the manifestation of the Spirit for the common good" (1 Corinthians 12:7). Whether these charisms be very remarkable or more simple and widely diffused, they are to be received with thanksgiving and consolation since they are primarily suited to and useful for the needs of the Church (*Lumen Gentium*, 12).

John Paul II, especially in his teaching on the vocation of the laity, repeatedly emphasized the universal outpouring of the Spirit's charisms upon all the faithful. These teachings call us to greater awareness of the variety of ordinary and extraordinary charisms and encourage our openness to whatever gifts the Spirit wishes to give. This teaching of the Second Vatican Council was accompanied by an outpouring of extraordinary and ordinary charisms among Catholics involved in the worldwide charismatic renewal and in many other movements of the Holy Spirit that emerged in the twentieth century.

## Charismatic Movements

Another way in which the Holy Spirit distributes charisms in the Church is when "the personal charism of some witnesses to God's love for men has been handed on" to their followers in the form of a new spiritual movement or community (*CCC* 2684). Each of these spiritual movements take from their founder some particular charism in the form of a specific way of living the Christian life, and they carry that charism forward as a distinctive charism of a religious community offering a particular spirituality and form of life to the wider Church. Saint Francis was described as an example of this in the previous chapter. We could add other examples here such as the charism of Saint Ignatius of Loyola handed on to the Jesuits and others, the charisms of Saint Teresa of Avila and Saint John of the Cross that reformed and continue to inspire the Carmelite orders; or the charism of Saint Josemaria Escriva, founder of *Opus Dei* along with other founders of lay movements in the Church. John Paul II describes how holiness or the perfection of love assumes many different concrete forms according to a person's unique conditions and his own "original way of self-giving." When this example of holiness is particularly strong, expressive, and original, it attracts others, and disciples gather to share in this unique personal charism that through the Holy Spirit gives birth to a new spiritual movement or community within the Church (8/10/1991).

In a gathering of many new lay movements in the Church on Pentecost Sunday in 1998, John Paul II spoke of the "charismatic dimension" of the Church (5/30/1998). John Paul II saw these new movements as fruit of the Second Vatican Council's "providential rediscovery" of the Church's charismatic dimension "as one of her constitutive elements." He described the charismatic dimension of the Church as "co-essential" with the institutional dimension. The Holy Spirit works in the history of the Church, not only through the ordained ministers and sacraments but also through the movements he inspires. These movements continue to release fresh spiritual energies in the life of the Church, bringing renewal and transformation to many within the Church. The various charisms of these movements provide multiple patterns of prayer and spiritual life whose rich diversity can be seen as many varied "refractions of the one pure light of the Holy Spirit" (*CCC* 2684).

## Criteria for Discerning Charisms

Discernment is necessary to authenticate those gifts that are genuine charisms, having their origin in the Holy Spirit. While the Spirit's presence in the saints is often confirmed by miracles, even extraordinary charisms are no guarantee of the presence of the Holy Spirit or the sanctity of the one who manifests those gifts. Jesus warned about those who perform miracles in his name but do not know him (Matthew 7:22–23). While we do not want to "quench the Spirit" we must "test the spirits" to know what is indeed inspired by the Holy Spirit (1 Thessalonians 5:19–21 and 1 John 4:1–2). Scripture and the catechism provide the following criteria for judging the authenticity of charisms and charismatic movements in the Church.

The first criterion is truth. Any supposedly inspired teaching, prophecy, vision, or other message, to be judged an authentic charism of the Holy Spirit, must conform to the truth of divine revelation given in Scripture and Tradition as interpreted by the magisterium of the Church. The charisms, if coming from the Holy Spirit, will not contradict what the Holy Spirit has revealed in Scripture, nor how he has led the Church. Most importantly, the Spirit confirms the truth about Jesus Christ. Thus, Saint John writes, "every spirit that confesses that Jesus Christ has come in the flesh is from God" (1 John 4:2), and Saint Paul says that no one speaking in the Spirit will deny Christ but rather it is through the Spirit that we are able to confess Jesus Christ as Lord (1 Corinthians 12:3). Likewise, the catechism reaffirms Jesus Christ as the Word and criterion by which all subsequent spiritual revelations must be judged (*CCC* 65–67).

Within the ongoing life of the Church, the pope and the bishops as successors to Peter and the apostles have received from Christ the authority and the grace to discern the authenticity of the charisms and to guide their practice. Thus, the catechism emphasizes that "no charism is exempt from being referred and submitted to the Church's shepherds" (*CCC* 801). These shepherds of the Church receive from the Holy Spirit the charism of truth (*CCC* 94, 890, 2035) by which they are able to discern his gifts among the people. Priests, too, are entrusted with the task of discerning the charisms of the laity. This is a positive task by which the shepherds, bishops, and priests encourage the laity in their response to the gifts and callings of the Holy Spirit and foster their collaboration in the mission of the Church. A humble and faithful submission to those whom the Holy Spirit has established as shepherds in the Church is a crucial sign of an authentic charism. John Paul II states quite plainly that the Holy Spirit does not inspire dissent or disobedience to those pastors whom the Holy Spirit himself has established in the Church (4/24/1991).

Submission to the pastors of the Church is an important means of realizing the second criterion of authentic charisms: the charisms are intended to serve the common good of the whole Church. The purpose of the charisms is to "directly or indirectly benefit the Church" (*CCC* 799). The Spirit distributes these special graces upon all the faithful for the "building-up of the Church" and for the "common good" of the whole Church (*CCC* 951). When Saint Paul seeks to guide the Corinthian Church in the proper use of the charisms, he reminds them that each one receives a charism for the "common good" and insists that "all things be done for building up" (1 Corinthians 12:7 and 14:26).

In order to promote the common good and the up-building of the whole Church, the charisms must meet the final and decisive criterion: love. In 1 Corinthians 13, right in the middle of Saint Paul's extended discourse on spiritual gifts, which runs from chapter 12—14 of that epistle, we find his most beautiful and poetic description of love:

If I speak in the tongues of mortals and of angels, but do not have love, I am a noisy gong or a clanging cymbal. And if I have prophetic powers, and understand all mysteries and all knowledge, and if I have all faith, so as to remove mountains, but do not have love, I am nothing…faith, hope, and love abide, these three; and the greatest of these is love. (1 Corinthians 13:1–2, 13).

Love represents the "more excellent way" and the "greater gifts" (1 Corinthians 12:31). The charisms must be exercised according to that Christ-like love, known in Greek as *agape* love, in Latin as *caritas*, in English as "charity." The catechism describes "charity" as "the true measure of all charisms" (*CCC* 800). Charisms, authentic promptings of the Holy Spirit, are to be received in gratitude as a rich grace for the whole Church and used in conformity to the love which that same Holy Spirit pours into our hearts.

## REFLECTION QUESTIONS

1. *What is the difference between the sanctifying gifts of the Holy Spirit and charisms of the Spirit?*

2. *How do the seven gifts of the Holy Spirit help us grow in holiness? Which gift have you experienced?*

3. *What are ordinary charisms? What ordinary charisms have you experienced or observed in others?*

4. *What are extraordinary charisms? What extraordinary charisms have you experienced or observed in others?*

5. *How do charisms help us to fulfill our vocations?*

6. *What criteria does the Church use to discern the authenticity of charisms?*

## The Writings of Blessed John Paul II

*The Holy Spirit in the Writings of Pope John Paul II.* Compiled by Father Bill Mc-Carthy. Saint Andrews Productions, 2001 (saintandrew.com). This is the most complete collection of John Paul II's writings on the Holy Spirit, including his encyclical on the Holy Spirit, the general audiences from the catechesis on the Spirit and the Year of the Holy Spirit, along with selected audiences from the catechesis on the Church, and a number of Pentecost homilies and addresses.

*The Spirit, Giver of Life and Love: Catechesis on the Creed, Vol. 3.* Pauline Books and Media, 1996. John Paul II's catechesis on the Spirit, 1989–1991.

*The Trinity's Embrace: God's Saving Plan: A Catechesis on Salvation History.* Pauline Books and Media, 2002. Includes John Paul II's general audiences for the Year of the Spirit in 1998.

John Paul II's general audience on Mary as the spouse of the Spirit, given on May 2, 1990, is missing from the collections above, but it may be found in Italian and Spanish among John Paul II's general audiences on the Vatican Web site (at the address given below) and is available in English as "God's Marital Love for Humanity" in *L'Osservatore Romano*, (English edition), May 7, 1990, p. 11.

The general audiences on theology of the body can be found in John Paul II's *Man and Woman He Created Them: A Theology of the Body*, translated by Michael Waldstein. Pauline Books and Media, 2006.

Most of the catechetical audiences are available in English on the Vatican Web site at vatican.va/holy_father/john_paul_ii/audiences/alpha/index_en.html

All of John Paul II's general audiences (although not all available in English) can be found on the Vatican Web site at vatican.va/holy_father/john_paul_ii/audiences/index.htm

**After John Paul II,** the writer I most recommend is Raniero Cantalamessa, an Italian Capuchin priest who has served as the preacher for the papal household under both John Paul II and Pope Benedict XVI. All of his books are recommended, but the most complete introductions to the Holy Spirit are found in the following books:

*Come, Creator Spirit: Meditations on the Veni Creator.* Liturgical Press, 2003.

*Sober Intoxication of the Spirit: Filled With the Fullness of God.* Servant Books, 2005.

# Also by John Gresham...

## Jesus 101
God and Man
**ISBN:** 978-0-7648-1931-5

"Christology is an expression of a deep love for Jesus Christ. Not only does Dr. Gresham demonstrate this in *Jesus 101*, he models it so we can follow him."

— Dr. Scott Hahn, professor of theology and Scripture
at Franciscan University of Steubenville

## Other Related Liguori Publications Titles

### The Living Church
Old Treasures, New Discoveries
*Christopher M. Bellitto*
**ISBN:** 978-0-7648-2039-7

Christopher M. Bellitto carefully explains how seven key elements developed through the centuries and became part of the Catholic tradition. *The Living Church* provides the historical context for the decisions, doctrine, and practice of the faith that were outlined in Bellitto's companion title, *Church History 101*. Bellitto introduces you to a living Church and takes you on a lively journey of faith that is as exciting today as any time in history.

### Church History 101
A Concise Overview
**ISBN:** 978-0-7648-1603-1

This easy-to-read volume answers the basic question, "what did the Church look like in this particular period?" for the four traditionally recognized eras of Church history: early, medieval, Reformation, and modern. Each chapter includes a map and timeline to locate the reader in time and place. All chapters conclude with discussion questions and a list for further reading.